QUICK PASCAL

QUICK PASCAL

DAVID L. MATUSZEK
The University of Tennessee

JOHN WILEY & SONS
New York • Chichester • Brisbane • Toronto • Singapore

Library of Congress Cataloging in Publication Data:

Matuszek, David L.
    Quick Pascal.

    Includes index.
    1. PASCAL (Computer program language)—Study and
teaching.   I. Title.
QA76.73.P2M35   1982   001.64'24   82-8354
ISBN 0-471-86644-X   AACR2

Printed in the United States of America

10 9 8 7 6 5 4 3 2 1

To My Father,
Chester Matuszek

PREFACE

The purpose of this book is to teach Pascal to programmers who need to know the language yesterday. It is not suitable for teaching Pascal to non-programmers. My intention is to make it practical to use Pascal in computer science courses even though students have not previously been taught this language.

The first chapter is an overview of Pascal and provides enough information for the student to be able to read most Pascal programs written by other people. The second chapter covers assorted details that the student will need to know in order to begin writing his or her own programs. Taken together, Chapters 1 and 2 provide a complete short course in Pascal. The remaining chapters are organized by topic, so that the student attempting to use a particular feature of Pascal (for example, variant records) will find all the necessary information in one place. This necessitates some redundancy; for example, all the information presented in Chapter 1 is repeated in greater detail at the appropriate places in later chapters. To further increase the value of the book as a reference, considerable summary information is provided in the appendices, and there is an extensive index.

The emphasis throughout the book is on teaching Pascal as it really is, not as it ought to be. Most Pascal books describe only an idealized "Standard Pascal," or else Pascal for a particular machine. This book describes not only Standard Pascal, but also four real implementations. Whatever dialect of Pascal you use, the chances are that it will be enough like one of these described here to enable you to find what you need. Throughout the book you will find hints for exploring the particular Pascal you are working with.

The language presented here is full Pascal; nothing from Standard Pascal has been left out, and many variations from Standard Pascal have been included, because Standard Pascal is certainly not what you have to work with on your machine.

Although Pascal is a useful language, it is not perfect. The quirks and problems you are likely to encounter are discussed in detail to help you get over the rough spots. The four representative implementations are

PASLC   The upper/lowercase compiler on the DEC-10, developed at the University of Hamburg, Germany.

Pascal 8000   The compiler for the IBM 360/370, developed at the University of Tokyo, Japan, by Teruo Hikita and Kiyoshi Ishihata for the Hitac 8800/8700 computer, and adapted for the IBM system by Gordon Cox and Jeffrey Tobias at the Australian Atomic Energy Commission, Australia.

CDC Pascal   The Pascal 6000-3.4 compiler for the CDC 6000 computers, as described by Kathleen Jensen and Niklaus Wirth.

UCSD Pascal   The Pascal compiler developed for use on microcomputers at the Institute for Information Science at the University of California at San Diego, under the direction of Kenneth L. Bowles (Apple version).

In this text we will refer to particular Pascal compilers by the above abbreviations. However, it should be understood that the companies that make these computers are not necessarily responsible for the Pascal compilers on those machines.

I thank Charles Hughes, Eugene Getchell III, and Hal Harrison for their careful reading of the manuscript. They caught many errors and made many helpful suggestions. Any errors that survive are, of course, entirely my own responsibility.

DAVID L. MATUSZEK

CONTENTS

PART ONE

INTRODUCTION

Chapter 1

AN OVERVIEW OF PASCAL

Pascal has become popular because it is a simple, easily understood language. In exchange for simplicity, it is less flexible than big languages like PL/I.

1.1 FIRST EXAMPLE: ADDING TWO NUMBERS

The fastest way to get familiar with the language is by looking at examples.

```
1   PROGRAM ADD (INPUT, OUTPUT);
2   (* EXAMPLE 1: Program to add two numbers. *)
3   VAR
4       I, J, SUM: INTEGER;
5   BEGIN
6   READ(I, J);
7   SUM := I + J;
8   WRITELN(SUM)
9   END.
```

The line numbers are not part of Pascal. They are there to help us discuss the example.

The first line names the program "ADD" and specifies the files (INPUT and OUTPUT) that it will use. INPUT is Pascal's name for the standard input file (regardless of what your operating system calls it) and OUTPUT is the name for the standard output file. INPUT and OUTPUT are examples of textfiles, that is, files which contain information in human-readable format (text). Pascal also supports the use of binary files.

Line 2 is a comment. Comments appear between the symbols (* and *). In some implementations and many textbooks you will also see comments enclosed between curly braces { and }. Comments may be put anywhere, except in the middle of a word or a number, or between the : and the = of the : = symbol.

In Pascal all declarations are put first, before any executable statements. In this program the declaration part is lines 3 and 4, and the executable part is lines 5 through 9.

All variables used in a program must be declared in a VAR part. Line 3 starts the VAR part; in line 4 the identifiers I, J, and SUM are declared to be integer variables. There are two types of numeric quantities in Pascal: INTEGERs (whole numbers) and REALs (which contain a decimal point). There is no default type—any variable you use, you must declare.

Some words in Pascal are reserved, that is, they cannot be used as variable names. The words VAR, BEGIN, and END in the above example are reserved words.

The executable body always starts with the keyword BEGIN (line 5) and ends with the word END followed by a period (line 9).

READ (line 6) is a call to a built-in procedure to read values from an input file and assign them to variables (in this case, I and J). WRITELN (line 8) is a built-in procedure to print out values.

The assignment statement (line 7) uses : = rather than = ; it says to set SUM to the sum of I and J. The symbol = means equality, not assignment, and is used in other places.

Semicolons (;) are used to separate one statement from the next, and one declaration from the next. In addition, there is a semicolon between the last declaration and the first BEGIN. This rule is conceptually simple, but difficult to apply; Section 2.2 gives some guidelines for placing semicolons.

PL/I programmers should note that semicolons are used differently in Pascal than in PL/I.

The example program is shown in all capital letters. On computer systems having lowercase letters as well, you can usually use either case, or mix them however you choose, and Pascal ignores the difference (except in quoted strings). Lowercase is easier for humans to read, and is preferable. This text uses all uppercase because so few machines provide lowercase.

Pascal is a free-format language. You do not need to start certain things in certain columns, or put exactly one statement per line. In fact, the Pascal compiler "sees" your program as one lone line, with the line boundaries and comments replaced by spaces. You could rewrite the above example as

```
PROGRAM ADD(INPUT,OUTPUT);
   (* EXAMPLE 1: Program to add two numbers. *)
```

```
VAR I,J,SUM:INTEGER;BEGIN READ(I,J);
SUM := I + J;WRITELN(SUM)END.
```

and the compiler would be just as happy (but your boss wouldn't).

Pascal is free-format in order to allow you to space and indent in such a way as to make your programs more readable. Increased readability will make your programs easier to debug and to maintain.

There are several different indentation schemes in vogue, and one can argue endlessly about the best way to indent. The scheme the author prefers is used throughout this text without further comment; but whatever indentation scheme is used should be followed consistently. Perhaps the least helpful indentation scheme is to start every line in the same column, as is often done in Fortran.

1.2   CONVENTIONAL DECLARATIONS IN PASCAL

This section describes those declarations in Pascal which should be familiar because they are similar to declarations in most other languages. All variables used in the program must be declared in the VAR section. Declarations have the following syntax,

   list_of_variables : *type*

where the *type* may be any of the following: INTEGER, REAL, CHAR (single character), BOOLEAN, or one of the other types in Pascal such as arrays. Variables of type CHAR may have as value any single character. Single character constants are written enclosed in single quote marks, for example, 'A'. BOOLEAN variables (called LOGICAL variables in Fortran) can take on either of the values TRUE and FALSE.

```
VAR
     I, J: INTEGER;                        (* two integer variables *)
     X, Y, Z: REAL;                        (* three real variables *)
     K: INTEGER;                           (* another integer variable *)
     CH: CHAR;                             (* a character variable *)
     P, Q, R: BOOLEAN;                     (* three boolean variables *)
     VEC: ARRAY [1..10] OF INTEGER;        (* see below *)
     BOX: ARRAY [1..10, -5..5] OF REAL;
```

VEC is declared to be a one-dimensional array of ten integers; those integers can be referenced by VEC[1], VEC[2], ..., VEC[10]. The notation 1..10 means that the allowable subscripts may range from one to ten, inclusive.

BOX is declared to be a two-dimensional array of real numbers. The first subscript can take on any value from one to ten inclusive, while the second subscript can take on any value from -5 to 5 inclusive. The elements are referred to in the program by BOX[1, −5], ..., BOX[10, 5]. Arrays may have any number of dimensions.

In Standard Pascal, there is no way to initialize variables. In Pascal 8000, however, variables may be initialized in the VALUE section, which must come after the VAR section. Every variable occurring in the VALUE section must previously have been declared in the VAR section. The syntax of an initialization is

> *variable* := *value*

(Note the use of : = rather than :.) For example,

```
VALUE
    X := 2.7929;
    CH := '*';
```

1.3   CONVENTIONAL STATEMENTS IN PASCAL

We have already seen examples of the assignment and the procedure call statements. (READ and WRITELN are procedure calls.) Here are some other Pascal statements.

IF *condition* THEN *statement*

> The *condition* is a Boolean expression, that is, an expression which results in a value of TRUE or FALSE. If the value of the *condition* is TRUE, then the *statement* is executed; otherwise it is not.

IF *condition* THEN *statement_1* ELSE *statement_2*

> If the value of the Boolean *condition* is TRUE, *statement_1* is executed; if the *condition* is FALSE, *statement_2* is executed.

WHILE *condition* DO *statement*

> This is a loop with the test at the top. The *condition* is evaluated; if TRUE, the *statement* is executed, and the program loops back to test the *condition* again. If FALSE, the loop exits, which means that control passes to the next statement. Note that if the *condition* is false initially, the loop exits immediately without ever having executed the *statement*.

REPEAT *sequence_of_statements* UNTIL *condition*

> This is a loop with the test at the bottom. The *sequence_of_statements* is executed first, then the *condition* is tested. If FALSE, the program loops back to execute the *sequence_of_statements* again; if TRUE, the loop exits.

Note three differences between the WHILE and REPEAT loops.

1 The body of the WHILE loop consists of a single statement, while the body of the REPEAT loop consists of a sequence of statements. You will soon see that this difference is not important.

2 The body of a WHILE loop may be executed zero times (that is, not at all), but the body of a REPEAT loop is always executed at least once.

3 The condition of a WHILE loop is false after the loop exists; the condition of a REPEAT loop is true after the loop exits.

There is reason to believe that REPEAT loops are harder to use and that people make more errors with them than with WHILE loops. Hence, all things being equal, you should prefer WHILE loops to REPEAT loops.

FOR *variable* := *initial_value* TO *final_value* DO *statement*

> This is a loop under count control. The *variable* is a simple unsubscripted variable; the *initial_value* and *final_value* can be any expressions resulting in a value of the same type as the *variable*. The loop executes the *statement* once for each of the values *initial_value* through *final_value*, with a step size of one. If the *initial_value* is greater than the *final_value*, the *statement* is never executed.

FOR *variable* := *initial_value* DOWNTO *final_value* DO *statement*

> This statement is like the preceding, except that the step size is minus one, rather than one. If the *initial_value* is less than the *final_value*, the *statement* is never executed.

Note that in all of the preceding statement types, the word *statement* refers to one single statement. Often it is desirable to use a sequence of statements, rather than just a single statement. The "fat parentheses" BEGIN and END make this possible.

BEGIN *sequence_of_statements* END

> BEGIN and END enclosing a *sequence_of_statements* form a single, compound statement. (Note that neither keyword by itself is a complete statement.)

Input/output in Pascal is trivially simple. Procedure READ takes any number of variable names as parameters, and reads that many values from the input; it can read integers, real numbers, or characters. Numeric values need not go in any particular columns, but must be separated by at least one space. READ treats a line boundary as if it were a space.

Procedure WRITELN takes any number of expressions as parameters, and writes out the value of those expressions on a single line. (Procedures WRITE and READLN also exist, but are less frequently used; see Section 8.3.)

1.4   SECOND EXAMPLE: SORTING AN ARRAY

```
1    PROGRAM SIMPLESORT (INPUT, OUTPUT);
2    (* This program reads in up to 100 integers, sorts them into ascending
3        order, and prints out the resultant array *)
4    VAR
5        A: ARRAY [1..100] OF REAL;
6        N: INTEGER; (* how many numbers *)
7        I: INTEGER;
8        TEMP: REAL;
9        SWAP: BOOLEAN;
10
11   BEGIN
12   (* read in how many numbers, then the numbers themselves *)
13   READ (N);
14   FOR I := 1 TO N DO READ (A[I]);
15   (* sort them by swapping (interchanging) adjacent numbers *)
16   SWAP := TRUE;   (* to get started, pretend a swap has occurred. *)
17   WHILE SWAP DO   (* continue looping until no more swaps occur. *)
18       BEGIN
19       SWAP := FALSE;
20       FOR I := 1 TO N − 1 DO   (* make one pass through the array. *)
21           IF A[I] > A[I + 1] THEN
22               BEGIN   (* two adj numbers out of order; swap them. *)
23                   TEMP := A[I]; A[I] := A[I + 1]; A[I + 1] := TEMP;
24                   SWAP := TRUE
25               END
26       END;
27   (* now write out the sorted array *)
28   FOR I := 1 TO N DO WRITELN (A[I])
29   END.
```

Line 1: Standard Pascal requires a PROGRAM line as the first line of every program. Some implementations (PASLC) do not have a PROGRAM statement, and will give you an error message if you try to use one.

The PROGRAM statement is of the form

PROGRAM *program_name* (*list_of_files*)

where *program_name* can be any identifier (it is never used again in the program), and *list_of_files* is a list of the names of all the files used by the program. INPUT and OUTPUT are the standard input and output files, respectively, and should be available on any Pascal implementation.

Lines 6 and 7: The two integer declarations could readily be combined into N, I: INTEGER, but were separated so that the comment would clearly refer only to N.

Line 10: Blank lines are legal and are very useful for separating major parts of the program.

Lines 13 and 14: READ ignores line boundaries, so it does not matter if the input data are on one line or many. Numbers on input are separated by one or more spaces, NOT by commas!

Lines 20 to 25: The body of the FOR loop is a single IF statement (albeit a complex one), hence does not require a BEGIN...END grouping. In contrast, the IF statement (lines 21 to 25) controls four assignment statements, so these must be grouped into a single compound statement.

Line 26: This END matches the BEGIN in line 18, so that lines 18 through 26 form the body of the WHILE loop started in line 17.

Line 28: WRITELN writes out the data followed by an end-of-line, so the result of executing N WRITELNs will be N lines, with one number per line.

1.5   PROCEDURES AND FUNCTIONS

Pascal procedures and functions are not compiled separately. They must be declared within any program in which they are to be used. Procedure and function declarations must come after all other declarations in a program.

The syntax of a procedure declaration is

```
PROCEDURE procedure_name ( parameter_list ) ;
    declarations;
    BEGIN
        procedure_body
    END
```

The *procedure_name* may be any valid identifier.

A procedure may have no parameters, in which case the parentheses are omitted. A procedure may use any variables declared in the main program. Parameters provide a means to call the procedure with different information in different places. For example, if you had a SORT procedure and two arrays *A* and *B*, you could call SORT (A) to sort array *A*, and SORT(B) to sort array *B*. Without parameters, your procedure would always have to sort the same array.

All parameters occurring in the *parameter_list* must have their types specified. The form of the specification resembles declarations in the VAR section; for example,

```
PROCEDURE WOW (I, J: INTEGER; X: REAL)
```

is the header for a procedure named WOW with three parameters, two of them integer and one real.

In a procedure header, the types of the parameters must be given by name. Type descriptions such as ARRAY [1..100] OF REAL are not allowed. (This restriction is removed in Pascal 8000.) Thus, for example, an array passed as a parameter must be given a type name in the TYPE section of the program (see Section 1.6), and that name must be used both for declaring variables to be passed to the procedure, and in the procedure header to specify any parameters of that type.

When the procedure is called, it must be called with the right number of parameters, in the right order, and the type names of the corresponding parameters must be identical.

Parameters are passed "by value." That is, when a procedure is called, the actual parameters (those used in the procedure call) are evaluated, and those values are assigned to the corresponding formal parameters (those given in the procedure header). The procedure may then assign to or otherwise alter the values of its formal parameters, but the actual parameters never get changed.

If it is intended that the procedure be allowed to change the values of one or more of the actual parameters so that information may be transmitted back to the calling program, those parameters may be specially marked, and will be passed by reference. Passing "by reference" means that the formal parameters will be treated as alternate names for the corresponding actual parameters. Anything done to the formal parameters in the procedure will really be done to the actual parameters. (In Fortran, all parameters are passed by reference.)

To pass parameters by reference, the special keyword VAR is put before those formal parameters. For example, in

PROCEDURE WOW (VAR I, J: INTEGER; X: REAL)

parameters I and J are passed by reference, and parameter X is passed by value. This use of the keyword VAR has nothing to do with the VAR section of declarations, and there is no obvious reason for Pascal to use this keyword in two completely different ways.

Declarations may be made inside a procedure. LABEL, CONST, TYPE, and VAR declarations (but not VALUE declarations, in Pascal 8000) may be made here; so may declarations of procedures and functions. In all cases, the meaning is that the declared entities are created when the procedure is entered, may be used inside the procedure, and disappear again when the procedure exits. Hence anything declared inside the procedure may be used inside the procedure, but cannot be used outside the procedure.

The body of a procedure is simply the sequence of executable statements which define the operation of that procedure. The procedure returns to its calling statement when the sequence of statements is finished; there is no explicit "return" statement.

A procedure is called simply by writing its name. Actual parameters, if any, are enclosed in parentheses. Actual parameters must match the formal parameters in order and type. Expressions may be used as actual parameters (except that it makes no sense to pass an expression by reference). For example, the following is a legal procedure call to WOW:

WOW (M, A[R, C],PI/2)

provided the types of the parameters are correct.

Functions are like procedures, except that they return a value. The type of the value returned is specified following the parameter list (if any). The syntax is

FUNCTION *function_name* (*parameter_list*) : *type*;
    declarations;
    BEGIN
       function_body
    END

where everything specified for procedures also holds for functions.

The *type* returned by a function must be specified by a name, not by a type description. Further, it must be the name of a simple type which can be returned in a register: it may be INTEGER, REAL, CHAR, or BOOLEAN, or one of the other simple types (subrange, pointer, or enumeration type) to be discussed in the next section.

The value to be returned by the function must be assigned to the function name, in an assignment statement of the form

function_name := *expression*

Any other use of the function name results in the function attempting to call itself. It is legal for procedures and functions to call themselves, but this should be done with care. (See Section 7.6.)

Functions are called by mentioning their names inside an expression; parameters, if any, are enclosed in parentheses.

FUNCTION LARGER (X, Y: REAL): REAL;
    BEGIN
       IF X > Y THEN LARGER : = X ELSE LARGER : = Y
    END;
. . .
A := 2 * LARGER(B/2, C) − 1

Functions, like procedures, may have VAR parameters, but this can lead to some rather subtle errors, hence is best avoided.

1.6 UNCONVENTIONAL FEATURES OF PASCAL

The features described in this section are unusual in that equivalent constructs do not necessarily exist in other, similar languages. In Pascal, however, these constructs are used regularly.

In addition to the VAR section of declarations, there are three other sections. The four sections are LABEL, CONST, TYPE, and VAR; they must appear in this order.

Any statement may be given a label; labeled statements may be branched to by GOTO statements. Labels are unsigned integer constants, and usually (depending on the compiler) must be declared in the LABEL section. The use of GOTO statements is discouraged in Pascal, hence labels are seldom used.

Constants may be declared in the CONST section. This is begun by the keyword CONST, and may contain any number of declarations of the form

identifer = *constant*

separated by semicolons. Following this declaration, the *identifier* is treated as a constant in all respects. It may be used anywhere a constant may be used, but it may not be altered by the program, nor used in any context where it could be altered. Its type is determined by the type of the *constant* which is its value. For example,

```
CONST
     PI = 3.1415926536;
     NCITIES = 20;
VAR
     POPULATION: ARRAY [1..NCITIES] OF INTEGER;
     DISTANCE: ARRAY[1..NCITIES, 1..NCITIES] OF REAL
```

New data types, based on existing data types, are declared in the TYPE section. The TYPE section begins with the keyword TYPE and contains any number of type declarations of the form

identifier = *type_description*

separated by semicolons. The *identifier* becomes the name of a new type (not the name of a variable) described by the *type_description*. For example,

```
TYPE
     STRG = ARRAY [1..80] OF CHAR
```

describes a new data type STRG. There do not yet exist any variables of type STRG; this is accomplished in the VAR section, that is,

```
VAR
     NAME, ADDRESS, OCCUPATION: STRG
```

defines three variables of type STRG. These variables may be referenced just as if they were declared to be of type ARRAY [1..80] OF CHAR directly.

In the above, ARRAY [1..80] OF CHAR is a "type description." The programmer may either declare this to be a new, named type (with the name STRG in this example) in the TYPE section or he may use the type description directly in the VAR section. In the latter case the type is an anonymous type, since it has not been given a name.

The following sections describe other ways in which the programmer can create new types in Pascal. In each case the syntax given will be for the type description, and may be used in either the TYPE section or the VAR section.

Enumeration Types

A scalar variable is one that can have as its value one of a fixed set of identifiers. BOOLEAN and CHAR variables are examples of scalar variables, because in each case there is a fixed, finite set of values of that type. INTEGER and REAL are not scalars because there are (in theory, at least) an infinite number of possible integer and real values.

Pascal allows the programmer to define his own scalar types by giving an exhaustive list of their possible values. These scalar types are called enumeration types. The type of such a variable is specified by the syntax

(*list_of_values*)

where the values in the *list_of_values* are written as simple identifiers. For example,

```
VAR
     YESTERDAY, TODAY, TOMORROW: (COLD, COOL, WARM, HOT)
```

describes three variables, each of which can take on any of the four values specified.

Enumeration variables and constants can be compared for equality and inequality: the first named in the *list_of_values* has the smallest value. The function ORD(*scalar_value*) returns the position of the enumeration value in the list, counting from zero; for example, ORD(WARM) has the value 2. SUCC(*scalar_value*) gives the next sequential value, and PRED(*scalar_value*) gives the preceding value; asking for the SUCCessor of the last value or the PREDecessor of the first value will result in a runtime error message. No textfile input/output is defined for enumeration types.

Subranges

A variable may be declared to take on values that are a subrange of the integers. The syntax is

least_value . . greatest_value

where *least_value* and *greatest_value* are integer constants. Any variable of type ''subrange of integer'' may be used as if it were an integer variable, but the Pascal compiler will generate (optional) runtime checks to ensure that its value remains within the stated range.

Variables may also be declared to be subranges of CHAR, of BOOLEAN, or of an enumeration type. Again, the only difference between subrange variables and other scalar variables is that the compiler may insert runtime checks to ensure that the values of subrange variables remain in the given range.

Records

Records are used to group data together. A record consists of a number of "fields". Each field is given a name, and the type of data which can be stored in that field is specified. The syntax of a record description is

```
RECORD
        list_of_field_names : type;
        list_of_field_names : type;
        . . .
        list_of_field_names : type        (* no ";" here *)
END
```

where *type* may be any type, even another record.

The individual field names are not used as if they were variable names, because there may be several records of the same type. Instead, both the name of the variable (of type record) and a field name for that kind of record must be used, separated by a dot ("."). An example will make this clearer.

```
TYPE
        DATE = RECORD
                        DAY: 1..31;
                        MONTH: 1..12;
                        YEAR: INTEGER
                END;
```

(* We have declared a new type DATE with three fields, DAY, MONTH, and YEAR, but we do not yet have any variables of type DATE. *)

```
VAR
        TODAY, MYBIRTHDAY, CHRISTMAS: DATE;
```

(* Now we have three variables of type DATE. Clearly we cannot just use, say, MONTH as a variable name, because there are three of them to choose from. *)

```
. . .
```

(* We can assign entire records, *)

```
MYBIRTHDAY := TODAY;
```

(* test entire records, *)

```
IF TODAY = MYBIRTHDAY THEN WRITELN(' HAPPY BIRTHDAY TO ME');
```

(* or deal with individual fields of a record. *)

```
TODAY.YEAR := 1982:
        IF (TODAY.MONTH = MYBIRTHDAY.MONTH) AND
                (TODAY.DAY < MYBIRTHDAY.DAY) THEN WRITELN(' SOON...')
```

Records can be tested for equality, but it is illegal to test whether one is larger or smaller than another. No textfile input/output is provided for whole records.

Records may have parts which vary. The variant part must come at the end of the record. It has the syntax

```
CASE tag : type_identifier OF
      case_label_list : ( field_list );
      case_label_list : ( field_list );
      . . .
      case_label_list : ( field_list )     (* no ";" *)
```

where the *tag* is just another field name, whose type is given by the *type_identifier*; each possible value of the *tag* is given in some one *case_label_list*; and each *field_list* specifies the fields that may be used in the record when the *tag* has one of the values in the attached *case_label_list*. There is no semicolon after the last *field_list* because this will be followed immediately by the END of the record.

For example, suppose that each record represents a machine-language instruction. Every instruction has an opcode and at least one register designator; some instructions have an address, while others have a binary flag and two additional register designators instead.

```
TYPE
      REGISTER = 0..7;
      INSTRUCTION = RECORD
          OPCODE: 0..255;
          R: REGISTER;
          CASE MEMORYREFERENCE: BOOLEAN OF
              TRUE: (ADDRESS: 0..65535);
              FALSE: (FLAG: BOOLEAN;
                        RX, RY: REGISTER)
      END;
```

The ADDRESS field of such a record should be used only when the MEMORYREFERENCE field is set to TRUE. The fields FLAG, RX, and RY should be used only when MEMORYREFERENCE is FALSE. The OPCODE and R fields may be used any time.

Pointers

Pointers are an advanced feature of Pascal. They are used to implement linked lists and other complex data structures. While the use of such data structures is beyond the scope of this book, this section and Chapter 12 will provide all the Pascal needed for building and manipulating linked data structures.

A pointer is a variable that "points to," or indicates, some other variable. If you know some machine language, you can think of a pointer as having a machine address as its value.

When you declare a pointer, you tell to what type of thing it is to point. You could have a "pointer to real," for example, which could point to one or another real number, but never to an integer. In practice, pointers almost always point to one kind or another of record.

The syntax of a pointer declaration is

↑ *type*

where *type* is the type of thing pointed to. It may be one of the fundamental types of Pascal (REAL, INTEGER, etc.), or it may be a type defined and given a name by the user in the TYPE section. It must, however, be the *name* of a type, and not the description of a type.

If P is a pointer variable declared above, then in the program P refers to the pointer itself, while P ↑ refers to the thing pointed to. There is one constant value for pointers, NIL, which means that nothing is pointed to. Pointers of the same type may be compared for equality, but not for relative size (greater or lesser), and they may be assigned. The procedure NEW(*pointer*) creates a new item of the type to which the *pointer* may point, and makes the *pointer* point to it; DISPOSE(*pointer*) destroys the item pointed to. No other operations are defined for pointers; in particular, no input or output is defined for pointers.

For example, given the declarations

```
TYPE
     NODE = RECORD
             VAL: INTEGER;
             NEXT: ↑NODE
          END;
VAR
     L, LAST: ↑NODE
```

the variables L and LAST are not NODEs, but only pointers to nodes. Their values are as yet undefined (and may be garbage). The statement

```
NEW(L)                          (* See Fig. 1.1 *)
```

creates a new NODE with fields VAL and NEXT; L is still not the name of

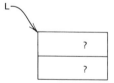

Fig. 1.1 Result of executing the call NEW(L). (The VAL field is shown on top; the NEXT field is shown on the bottom.) Both fields may contain garbage.

the node, but merely points to it. To refer to the node itself you must use
L ↑ . For example,

L ↑ .VAL := 1;   (* See Fig. 1.2 *)

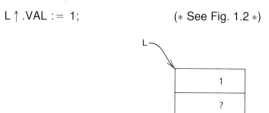

Fig. 1.2 Result of executing the statement
L↑.VAL := 1 .

LAST := L;   (* See Fig. 1.3 *)

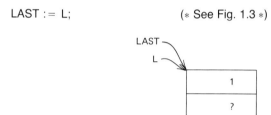

Fig. 1.3 Result of executing the statement
LAST := L. The pointer value in L is simply
copied to LAST, so both variables now point to the
same node.

NEW(LAST ↑ .NEXT);   (* See Fig. 1.4 *)

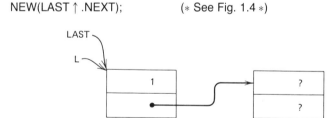

Fig. 1.4 Result of executing the call NEW(LAST ↑ .NEXT) . The pointer given to
NEW need not be a simple variable; here it is a field of the record pointed to by
LAST.

LAST := LAST ↑ .NEXT;   (* See Fig. 1.5 *)

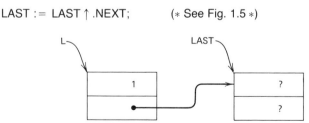

Fig. 1.5 Result of executing the statement LAST := LAST↑.NEXT . LAST has
been "stepped along" to the next node in the list.

LAST ↑ .VAL := 2;   (∗ See Fig. 1.6 ∗)

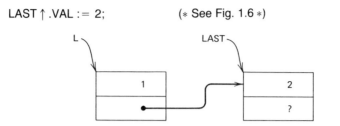

Fig. 1.6 Result of executing the statement LAST ↑ .VAL := 2 .

LAST ↑ .NEXT := NIL;   (∗ See Fig. 1.7 ∗)

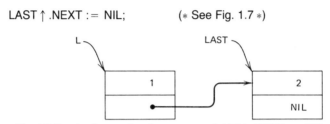

Fig. 1.7 Result of executing the statement LAST ↑ .NEXT := NIL . This marks
the node LAST ↑ as being the last node in the list.

and so on. A second call of NEW(L) will create a new node, and in the
process will lose track of the first one, so before doing this you may wish
either to make a copy of the pointer (by doing L2 := L, where L2 is the same
type of pointer as L), or to return L for recycling (with DISPOSE(L)) so that
the memory space for the first node L ↑ is available for reuse.

Sets

Pascal has a data type called a SET which resembles a set as the term is
defined in mathematics. Pascal severely limits the types of items that may be
in a set, and omits some of the commonly used set operations.

The syntax of a set description is

SET OF *type*

where *type* may be an enumeration type, a subrange of integer, a subrange of
character, BOOLEAN, or (sometimes) CHAR. The set may contain any or
all of the values of that type; it represents not a single value, but a group of
values. For example, a SET OF 0..10 may contain, at some given instant, the
four values 2, 5, 6, and 10.

The elements of a set are limited by the implementation technique to
small integers or other things which may be represented by small integers.
The largest integer in the set determines the maximum number of elements
that may be in the set. Typical limits are PASLC, 0..71; Pascal 8000, 0..63;
CDC, 0..58; UCSD Pascal, 0..511. The range is too small to allow SET OF
CHAR, except in UCSD Pascal.

The following operations are defined on sets.

+	set union
*	set intersection
−	set difference
=, <>	set equality, set inequality
<=, >=	subset test, superset test
e IN *s*	test whether *e* is an element of *s*
:=	set assignment.

Set values may be written with square brackets, for example, [1, 2, 3], [1..5, 10, 15..20], [ ], or [I, I+1]. No input/output is provided for sets, nor (except in Pascal 800) is there any way to sequence through all the elements of a set.

Packed Structures

Array, record, set, and file declarations may be preceded by the keyword PACKED. This is a request to the compiler to minimize the storage space required by those structures, usually at the expense of less efficient access to their parts.

```
TYPE
      BYTE = PACKED ARRAY[0..7] OF BOOLEAN;
      WORD = PACKED RECORD
            LSB, MSB: BYTE
      END
```

Case Statements

A CASE statement is a means of selecting one statement to be executed, out of a number of statements, according to the value of some expression. The syntax is

```
CASE expression OF
      list_of_values :
            statement;
      list_of_values ;
            statement;
      . . .
      list_of_values :
            statement     (* no ";" here *)
END
```

where the values in each *list_of_values* must all be constants, and must all be of the same type (the type of the *expression*).

Execution is as follows. The *expression* is evaluated, and its value is searched for the *list_of_values* parts. When the value is found, the single *statement* following it is executed; control then passes to the next statement (if any) following the END.

The type of the *expression* (and the constant values) must be a simple type other than REAL, that is, it must be INTEGER, CHAR, BOOLEAN, enumeration, or subrange. REAL is not allowed because approximation and roundoff errors make it poor practice ever to test two real numbers for exact equality.

If the value of the *expression* does not occur as the prefix to any *statement* in the CASE statement, the result is undefined (anything can happen). Pascal 8000 fixes this by allowing the word ELSE to prefix the final *statement*, so that if the value is not found, the final *statement* will be executed. PASLC has the same feature, but uses the word OTHERS rather than ELSE. UCSD Pascal does not provide an ELSE or OTHERS, but simply defines the CASE statement to do nothing if the value of the *expression* is not found in any *list of values*.

As usual, BEGIN and END may be used to group a sequence of statements together into a single statement.

WITH Statements

When working extensively with a single record, the dot notation described earlier can get annoyingly lengthy. The WITH statement allows the programmer to use the field names of a record as if they were variable names, without naming the particular record every time. The syntax is

WITH *record_variable* DO *statement*

so that, for example, the following statement sequences are equivalent.

```
TODAY.DAY := 16;        WITH TODAY DO
TODAY.MONTH := 1;         BEGIN
TODAY.YEAR := 1982        DAY := 16;
                          MONTH := 1;
                          YEAR := 1982
                        END
```

1.7   THIRD EXAMPLE: COUNTING A BRIDGE HAND

The following program reads in a Bridge hand and counts its value. In case you do not play Bridge, the rules are:

  1 A Bridge hand consists of 13 cards randomly selected from a standard 52 card deck.

  2 Aces are worth 4 points, Kings 3, Queens 2, and Jacks 1. Other cards do not count.

3 A void (no cards) in any suit is worth 3 points; a singleton (just one card in a suit) is worth 2 points; and a doubleton (just two cards in a suit) is worth one point.

4 Deduct one point for any singleton King, Queen, or Jack, or for a Queen or Jack in a doubleton with a small (2..10) card.

Input will consist of thirteen card specifications separated by blanks. Each card specification will consist of one or two characters giving its value (2, 3, ..., 10, J, Q, K, A) and one giving its suit (C, D, H, S). For example,

5D 2H JC 10H 9D 4S AS 3D 9C KH 5H 4D JD

Only the 10 cards such as 10H require three characters for their representation, so inside the program we will ignore the '0' and represent a 10 by the character '1'. This will cause no confusion because an ace is represented in the input data by an 'A', not by its numerical value.

In reading a Pascal program, it is usually best to proceed in a top–down fashion, by locating and reading the main program first, referring to the declarations as needed. As you read the main program, try to understand it without reference to the procedures and functions it calls; instead, make reasonable assumptions about what they must do. Then, having read the main program, locate each procedure and function it calls, and read them the same way.

With practice, this way of reading a program is faster than reading it front to back, like a book. It is also the best order in which to write a program.

```
PROGRAM BRIDGEHAND (INPUT, OUTPUT);
    (* Read in and count a single Bridge hand. *)
TYPE
    SUITNAME = (CLUB, DIAMOND, HEART, SPADE);
    CARD = RECORD
            VAL: CHAR;
            SUIT: SUITNAME
    END;
    HAND = ARRAY [1..13] OF CARD;
VAR
    MYHAND: HAND;
    POINTS: INTEGER;


PROCEDURE READCARD (VAR CD: CARD);
    (* Read one Playing card. No error checking is done. *)
    VAR
        CH: CHAR;
    BEGIN
        REPEAT READ(CH) UNTIL CH <> ' '; (* skip blanks *)
        CD.VAL:=CH;
```

```
IF CH = '1' THEN READ (CH); (* ignore the '0' in '10' *)
READ(CH);
CASE CH OF
      'C': CD.SUIT:=CLUB;
      'D': CD.SUIT:=DIAMOND;
      'H': CD.SUIT:=HEART;
      'S': CD.SUIT:=SPADE
   END
END;


PROCEDURE READHAND (VAR H: HAND);
   (* Read one hand of cards. No error checking is done. *)
   VAR
      I: INTEGER;
   BEGIN
      FOR I:=1 TO 13 DO READCARD(H[I])
   END;


FUNCTION HIGHCARDS (H: HAND): INTEGER;
   (* Count the high card points in hand H. *)
   VAR
      I, POINTS: INTEGER;
   BEGIN
      POINTS:=0;
      FOR I:=1 TO 13 DO
         CASE H[I].VAL OF
            '1', '2', '3', '4', '5', '6', '7', '8', '9': ;
                  (* empty statement—does nothing *)
            'J': POINTS:=POINTS+1;
            'Q': POINTS:=POINTS+2;
            'K': POINTS:=POINTS+3;
            'A': POINTS:=POINTS+4
         END;
      HIGHCARDS:=POINTS
   END;


FUNCTION DISTRIBUTION (H: HAND): INTEGER;
   (* Count distribution points, deducting for unprotected
      high cards. *)
   VAR
      SUITCOUNT: ARRAY [SUITNAME] OF INTEGER;
      I, POINTS: INTEGER;
      S: SUITNAME;
      LOWCARD, JACKORQUEEN: BOOLEAN;
   BEGIN
      (* Count number of cards in each suit. *)
```

```
FOR S: = CLUB TO SPADE DO SUITCOUNT[S]: = 0;
FOR I: = 1 TO 13 DO
      SUITCOUNT[H[I].SUIT]: = SUITCOUNT[H[I].SUIT] + 1;
(* Count points for voids, singletons, and doubletons. *)
POINTS: = 0;
FOR S: = CLUB TO SPADE DO
      IF SUITCOUNT[S] < 3 THEN
            POINTS: = POINTS + 3 − SUITCOUNT[S];
(* Deduct for singleton Jack, Queen, or King. *)
FOR I: = 1 TO 13 DO
      IF (H[I].VAL IN [ 'J', 'Q', 'K']) AND
      (SUITCOUNT[H[I].SUIT] = 1) THEN
            POINTS: = POINTS − 1;
(* Deduct for doubleton Queen or Jack. *)
FOR S: = CLUB TO SPADE DO
      IF SUITCOUNT[S] = 2 THEN
            BEGIN
            LOWCARD: = FALSE;
            JACKORQUEEN: = FALSE;
            FOR I: = 1 TO 13 DO
                  IF H[I].SUIT = S THEN
                        IF H[I].VAL IN ['J', 'Q'] THEN
                              JACKORQUEEN: = TRUE
                        ELSE IF H[I].VAL IN ['1'.. '9'] THEN
                              LOWCARD: = TRUE;
                  IF LOWCARD AND JACKORQUEEN THEN
                        POINTS: = POINTS − 1
            END;
      DISTRIBUTION: = POINTS
END;

FUNCTION HANDCOUNT (H: HAND): INTEGER;
      (* Count the hand. *)
      BEGIN
            HANDCOUNT: = HIGHCARDS(H) + DISTRIBUTION(H)
      END;

BEGIN (* -------- MAIN PROGRAM -------- *)
READHAND(MYHAND);
WRITELN(' My hand contains', HANDCOUNT(MYHAND), ' points.')
END.
```

Chapter 2

ISSUES IN
WRITING PASCAL
PROGRAMS

It has been said that "the Devil hides in the details." This section contains a potpourri of details, none of them profound, but any of which may frustrate your attempts to produce a working program.

2.1 LEXICAL ISSUES

The Character Set

Some computers do not have all the characters used by Pascal in their character sets and must make substitutions. Some implementations have the characters available, but make substitutions anyway. The table on the next page summarizes these substitutions.

The character set used in this book is that of Standard Pascal, with three exceptions. First, features unique to Pascal 8000 are shown using the Pascal 8000 character set. Second, because the standard comment delimiters { and } are seldom used in practice, even when available, this book follows the common practice of using (* and *) instead. Third, it has been necessary for typographical reasons to use both 'and' to represent the (one) single quote character of Pascal.

Your computer may have lowercase letters. If it does, then you can certainly use lowercase letters as character data and in quoted strings. However, your compiler may or may not be written to allow you to use

STANDARD PASCAL	CDC 6000 PASCAL	PASCAL 8000	DEC-10 PASCAL	UCSD PASCAL
[ ]	[ ]	(. .)	[ ]	[ ]
{ }	(* *)	(* *)	{}, (* *)	{}, (* *)
↑	↑	@	^	^
<>	≠	<>	#	<>
<=	≤	<=	<=	<=
>=	≥	>=	>=	>=
,	≡	,	,	,
AND	&	AND	AND	AND
OR	∨	OR	OR	OR
NOT	¬	NOT	NOT	NOT

lowercase in keywords, for example, if, while, begin) and in programmer-defined names, (for example, max, count).

In those implementations where lower case can be used in keywords and identifiers, case differences are ignored. Thus, "MAXVAL," "maxval," and "MaxVal" are different ways of writing the same name. PASLC follows this convention; other implementations are supposed to, but may not.

Names and Keywords

Programmer-defined names must begin with a letter and must consist entirely of letters and digits. In PASLC and UCSD Pascal, both upper and lowercase may be used in names, but no distinction is made between the two cases: names are stored internally as all uppercase. In Pascal 8000, $ and _ (the dollar sign and the underscore) are considered to be letters. UCSD Pascal and PASLC allow underscores within names. There is no limit on the length of names, but Standard Pascal requires the compiler to pay attention only to the first eight characters; it may ignore the rest.

Pascal keywords are reserved, and you may not use them as names. For example, it is illegal to name a variable IF. The complete list of keywords is

AND	DOWNTO	IF	OR	THEN
ARRAY	ELSE	IN	PACKED	TO
BEGIN	END	LABEL	PROCEDURE	TYPE
CASE	FILE	MOD	PROGRAM	UNTIL
CONST	FOR	NIL	RECORD	VAR
DIV	FUNCTION	NOT	REPEAT	WHILE
DO	GOTO	OF	SET	WITH

FORWARD is not a reserved word in Standard Pascal, although most compilers treat it as one. Other words which are not reserved are IN-TEGER, REAL, CHAR, BOOLEAN, READ, READLN, WRITE,

WRITELN, INPUT, OUTPUT, and the names of the standard functions. In UCSD Pascal the words EXTERNAL, FORWARD, IMPLEMENTA-TION, INTERFACE, SEGMENT, UNIT, and USES are reserved. In Pascal 8000 the words FORALL, LOOP, POSTLUDE, and VALUE are reserved.

Blanks or other delimiters are required around both keywords and programmer-defined names. For example,

FORI: = 1TO10DOA[I]: = 0   (∗ illegal ∗)

is illegal as well as unreadable. Usually any character other than a letter or a digit can serve as a delimiter, so that

IF(X<Y)AND(Y<Z)THEN WRITELN(X,Y,Z)

is legal, if a bit crowded. Comments and newline characters also serve as delimiters.

The other side of the coin is that delimiters may not occur within a name, number, or keyword. Unless you are one of those programmers who tries to pack everything into as small a space as possible, the spacing you normally use will work just fine.

Numbers and Numeric Expressions

Numbers may not contain delimiters such as blanks or commas. If a number contains a decimal point, then there must be digits on both sides of the decimal point: .5 and 1. are not allowed.

Standard Pascal does not have an exponentiation operator. See Section 4.1 for exponentiation routines you can use. Pascal 8000 uses ∗∗ for exponentiation, and it is right associative, that is, $X**Y**Z$ is computed as $X**(Y**Z)$.

The order of precedence of arithmetic operators is the usual one, with exponentiation first (when available), then multiplication and division, then addition and subtraction, then comparisons (= , <, etc.) last. However, the precedence of the Boolean operators AND, OR, and NOT is badly chosen (see Section 4.4), so it is best always to use parentheses with these operators to make the desired order of evaluation explicit.

2.2   SEMICOLONS

If you already know Algol 60 or one of its descendents (Simula, Jovial, Algol 68, etc.), then skip this section, as the rules for semicolons are exactly the same in Pascal. If you know PL/I which uses semicolons differently, or if you know some language which does not use semicolons, then read on.

In Pascal, the key idea is that semicolons go between things. They separate one thing from the next. In the declaration section, semicolons go between declarations. In the executable portion, semicolons go between statements which are at the same level of nesting. There is also a semicolon between the last declaration and the first BEGIN of the executable portion. Since semicolons are only separators, it follows that there is no semicolon before the first statement in a sequence, or after the last statement in a sequence.

In Pascal, BEGIN and END are not two different statements; rather, they are the beginning and ending keywords of a single statement, called a "compound statement." Often BEGIN and END are spoken of as "fat parentheses," since they behave exactly like parentheses, having no function other than to group things.

For example,

```
IF A < B THEN
    A := A + 1
ELSE
    BEGIN
    A := A - 1;
    B := B + 1
    END;
WRITELN (X, Y)
```

The statement $A := A + 1$ is preceded by THEN and followed by ELSE, neither of which are statements. Similarly, $A := A - 1$ is preceded by BEGIN, and $B := B + 1$ is followed by END, which are not statements. However, $A := A - 1$ and $B := B + 1$ are separated by a semicolon, and a semicolon is used to separate the IF statement (which here ends with the word END) from the WRITELN which follows it.

One way of stating the rule is that at the end of a statement, if there is another statement immediately following at the same level of nesting, you need a semicolon. If the next thing after the statement is only part of a statement (such as ELSE or END) at some higher level of nesting, you do not need a semicolon.

Continuing the analogy with parentheses, suppose you wanted to group three items, say A, B, and C. You might write (A, B, C), using commas as separators, but you would not write (, A, B, C,). Similarly you can group three statements S1, S2, and S3 as

```
BEGIN S1; S2; S3 END
```

where semicolons separate statement from statement, but not statement from fat parenthesis.

Actually, you can often get away with excess semicolons, because Pascal allows a so-called "empty statement," which does nothing. For example, in

BEGIN; S1; S2; S3; END

there are five statements grouped together, of which the first and last are empty. This is legal and harmless, but poor form.

Not all excess semicolons are harmless, however. Consider the two statements

IF *condition* THEN *statement*

and

IF *condition* THEN *statement_1* ELSE *statement_2*.

In the second form of IF statement, a semicolon after *statement_1* will change it into the first form of IF statement; the semicolon indicates that this statement has ended and another statement will follow. The next statement, however, would begin with the keyword ELSE, and there is no such thing as an ELSE statement in Pascal. The keyword pairs REPEAT...UNTIL and CASE...END also bracket sequences of statements, and the same rules for semicolons apply to these as to BEGIN...END.

There is an additional problem with CASE...END. These keywords enclose not simply a sequence of statements, but rather a sequence of labeled statements in which the labels are the values which may be assumed by the case expression. In this context an unlabeled statement is not legal, hence an empty statement resulting from an excess of semicolons is not legal either. The compiler is likely to give a rather mysterious message about a missing or illegal label, but is not likely to mention semicolons.

Finally, one rule that may be found helpful is never to use a semicolon before an END or an ELSE. This rule always applies, and protects from the errors mentioned above; if you do not mind having a few unnecessary empty statements, it may be adequate for your needs.

2.3   ONE-PASS COMPILATION

Pascal is designed so that it can be implemented by a one-pass compiler. A one-pass compiler is a compiler that translates the program as it goes along, never going back to change something that it has already translated. Since Pascal requires that all names are declared before they are used, this leads to a few minor problems.

Declarations must be in the order LABEL, CONST, TYPE, VAR, VALUE (Pascal 8000 only), then all procedures and functions. This ordering is not wholly arbitrary.

You may wish to use constants (declared in the CONST section) in the TYPE and VAR sections. You will almost certainly want to use the names of new types (declared in the TYPE section) in the VAR section. If you are using Pascal 8000, you can hardly assign initial values to variables in the VALUE section unless those variables have already been declared in the VAR section. Because of the ordering of these sections you can do all these things, yet still get the efficiency of a one-pass compiler.

Procedures and functions may not be called before they are defined. This means that you will have to arrange your routines so that this condition is met. If this cannot be done, either because you have mutually recursive routines (routines that call each other), or simply because you have other ideas about how to order routines, you can break each routine up into two parts: the first part consisting of the complete routine header, but with the keyword FORWARD replacing the body of the routine, and the second part with an abbreviated header (giving no parameter list or return type) followed by the real body. For example,

```
FUNCTION DOUBLE (I: INTEGER): INTEGER;
    FORWARD;
. . .
(* Other intervening functions and procedures *)
. . .
FUNCTION DOUBLE;
    BEGIN
        DOUBLE:=2*I
    END
```

A final note concerning error messages: Almost all Pascal compilers are written in such a way as to given error messages as soon as possible, when it is first discovered that an error has occurred, and to provide a pointer to the symbol being processed at the time. This is not necessarily the same as pointing at the error itself, which is often but not always the immediately preceding symbol. For example,

```
IF X<Y THEN X:=X+1;
ELSE X:=X-1;
    ↑ error
```

Here the actual error is presumably the semicolon which terminates the IF statement. To the compiler, however, an IF statement without an ELSE part is perfectly legal; the error is that no legal statement can begin with the keyword ELSE.

The actual error is ALWAYS at or before the error marker, NEVER after it. If your program happens to have comments just before the error message occurs, remember that these comments are invisible to the compiler (except for acting as delimiters), and that the "real" error may be just before the comments.

Comments not closed properly can cause large portions of code to be ignored. For example, if you accidentally type (* some comment $), then everything up to and including the next *) becomes part of the comment. If you are working from a printed listing of your program, there will typically be additional information printed to the left of your Pascal code, which can help you spot errors of this type.

2.4   COMPILER OPTIONS

A compiler option is a request to do or not to do certain things when compiling. The options are specified within the Pascal program itself, by a special comment of the form

(*$*options comment*)*

An *option* usually consists of a single letter fcllowed by a plus or a minus sign. A plus means to turn the option on, and a minus means to turn it off. Options are separated by commas. The *comment* may be any text, but it is usually omitted.

Specific options differ widely from one version of Pascal to the next. Typical compiler options include

- List the Pascal source program;
- List the object code produced;
- Compile only the first 72 columns of each line;
- Increase the stack size;
- Reset the size of the buffers;
- Insert runtime checks for assorted errors;

and so forth. Unfortunately, compiler options vary so greatly from one implementation to the next that we cannot supply any generally useful list. Appendix D contains very brief summaries of the options for the four representative implementations discussed in this book, but even these can vary.

PART TWO

DECLARATIONS AND STATEMENTS

Chapter 3

DECLARATIONS

In Pascal, all identifiers must be declared. There are five sections of declarations (six in Pascal 8000). Sections are omitted if there are no identifiers of that type to be declared. Each section is introduced by a particular keyword except the section of procedures and functions. Sections that are present must occur in the following order.

LABEL   Statements may have labels that are unsigned integers; all labels must be declared (except in PASLC).

CONST   Identifiers may be assigned permanent values in this section. The values of such identifiers cannot be altered by the program; they may be used wherever literal constants may be used, as, for example, in declaring array bounds.

TYPE   New types may be named in this section.

VAR   Variables are declared in this section.

VALUE   (Pascal 8000 only) Variables may be given initial values at compilation time.

....   All procedures and functions are declared in this final section, which is not introduced by a specific keyword.

3.1   THE LABEL SECTION

Any statement may have a label. A label is an integer in the range 0 to 9999, and is followed by a colon. All labels must be declared in the LABEL section (except in PASLC, which has labels but no LABEL section).

```
LABEL
      1, 2, 3, 17, 50, 33;
```

Leading zeroes are allowed (up to four digits total) but are ignored. Zero (0) may be used as a label. Labels obey the same scope rules as any other identifier (see Section 7.3).

The purpose of labeling a statement is to allow another statement to jump to it by means of a GOTO statement. For example,

```
        I := 1;
17:     IF I > N THEN GOTO 33;
        A[I] := 0;
        I := I+1;
        GOTO 17;
33:     ;                          (* labeled empty statement *)
```

A statement which contains other statements (for example, a WHILE loop or an IF statement) is said to be "structured." It is legal in most Pascals to label and jump to statements embedded in a structured statement, but the subsequent behavior of the structured statement is undefined—do not do it!

It is illegal to jump into a procedure or function from outside of it. It is legal (except in UCSD Pascal) to jump out of a procedure or function, but this is not a good practice.

It is generally agreed that GOTO statements (and statement labels) should not be used. Pascal provides them for those rare instances in which they may be necessary. Normally, however, the GOTO statement is only found necessary by programmers used to a programming language (such as Fortran or Basic) which has a weak set of control structures, or who are used to flowcharting first and then constructing programs based on the flowchart.

Traditional flowcharting techniques are not well-suited to Pascal because flowcharts can use arbitrarily tangled control structures which cannot readily be translated into Pascal. If you prefer to flowchart before coding, there are several newly developed "structured flowcharting" techniques that you may wish to investigate.

Both Fortran and flowcharts allow the user to build complex, tangled control structures which are not readily coded in Pascal. The programmer who is addicted to such control structures has two choices. (1) He can learn to use the simple control structures of Pascal (which really are sufficient for his needs), thus improving the quality of his code substantially; (2) He can learn how to use Boolean variables as flags to create equally tangled control structures in Pascal.

3.2   THE CONST SECTION

Identifiers may be given permanent values in the CONST section. The format of a constant declaration is *identifier = value*

where *value* is one of

1 An integer or real number (with or without a sign).

2 An identifier previously declared as a constant (if numeric, may be prefixed by a sign).

3 A quoted single character.

Example:

```
CONST
      ONE = 1;
      MINUSONE = −1;
      PI = 3.1415926536;
      MINUSPI = −PI;
      BLANK = ' ';
```

Note that the equals sign is used here. The CONST establishes an exact identity between the value and the identifier, so that the identifier may be used exactly as if (and only as if) it were the literal value itself.

In Pascal 8000 the *value* part may also be

4 A quoted string (also available in UCSD Pascal).

5 A constant of type SET, with set elements enclosed in square-bracket substitutes (. and .).

6 An array constant or record constant, with its component values enclosed in the symbols (# and #), followed by a description of that array or record.

Examples:

```
COPYRIGHT    = 'COPYRIGHT (C) 1982 BY DAVID MATUSZEK';
NONPRIMES    = (. 6, 8..10, 12, 14..16, 18, 20 .);
NULLVECTOR   = (# 0.0, 0.0 #): ARRAY(.1..2 .) OF REAL;
COMPLEXZERO = (# 0.0, 0.0 #):
      RECORD
            RE, IM: REAL
      END;
```

No arithmetic or other operations are allowed in the CONST section; the above examples virtually exhaust the possibilities.

Proper use of the CONST section can greatly enhance the flexibility of programs. For example, rather than declaring an array to be of size 100 and running all loops to 100, one could write instead:

```
CONST
      ARRAYSIZE = 100;
VAR
```

A: ARRAY [1..ARRAYSIZE] OF INTEGER;
. . .
FOR I := 1 TO ARRAYSIZE DO
    . . .

If the programmer can use the constant name consistently throughout the program, instead of using its intended value, a subsequent change to the array size can be made by changing only a single CONST definition. One trick that can aid in attaining this consistency is to not decide on the value of the array size (or other constant) until after the program is written. It has even been argued that constants should never be allowed to occur in the body of the program. This is an extreme view, but contains some truth.

3.3   THE TYPE SECTION

In the TYPE section data types are given names. The format of a type declaration is

type_name = *type*

where the *type* may be either the name of a previously defined type, or it may be the description of a type such as an array or record description.

Pascal requires that in an assignment statement, the value to the right of the := must be of the same type as the variable being assigned to. In addition, in a call of a function or procedure, the types of the actual parameters must match those of the corresponding formal parameters. Both of these requirements assume some notion of type equivalence, that is, of deciding when two variables have the "same" type.

Broadly speaking, there are two different notions of what it means for two types to be the same. The first, called "name equivalence," is that two types are the same if they have the same name. The second, "structural equivalence," is that two types are the same if they have the same types of components, with the same component names (in the case of records), in the same order.

Standard Pascal uses name equivalence, which is faster and easier for the compiler. Pascal 8000 uses primarily structural equivalence, which is usually closer to what the programmer thinks of as the same.

To get some idea of the difference, consider these declarations.

VAR
    A, B: ARRAY [1..5, 1..10] OF REAL;
    C: ARRAY [1..5, 1..10] OF REAL;
    D: ARRAY [1..5] OF ARRAY [1..10] OF REAL;

Which of these are the same type? Under structural equivalence, they are all the same, including D. Under name equivalence, the compiler would consider A and B both to be of anonymous type #1, hence the same, but C would be anonymous type #2, and D would be anonymous type #3. Hence there are three different types in use above.

The primary purpose of the TYPE section is therefore to give names to types, so that anonymous types can be avoided. This is particularly important for assignments and parameter transmission.

Under either definition of type equivalence, there are problems. One prominent problem is that, under either definition, two arrays of different sizes are of different types. This means, for example, that you cannot write a sort routine that can sort either of two arrays which differ in length. You must have a separate sort routine for each type of array.

The CONST and TYPE declarations provide some relief for this problem. For example,

```
CONST
     ARRAYSIZE = 100;
TYPE
     ARRAYTYPE = REAL;
     SORTABLEARRAY = ARRAY [1..ARRAYSIZE] OF ARRAYTYPE;
. . .
PROCEDURE SORT (VAR A: SORTABLEARRAY);
     (* Procedure to sort location 1..ARRAYSIZE of A *)
     . . .
```

Note that this sort procedure has the same restrictions as any other sort procedure in Pascal: it sorts only an array of exactly 100 real numbers. It can, however, be pulled out and used again in some other program that defines ARRAYSIZE and ARRAYTYPE differently; when it is recompiled, it will do only that particular sorting job.

Declarations of arrays, records, sets, and files may be preceded by the keyword PACKED. PACKED indicates to the compiler that storage used for the structure must be minimized (usually by packing more than one element per word).

```
TYPE
     INSTRUCTION = PACKED RECORD
          OPCODE: 0..63;
          INDIRECTBIT: BOOLEAN;
          DISPLACEMENT: -256..255
     END;
     BYTE = PACKED ARRAY [0..7] OF BOOLEAN;
```

Packed structures require less space, but the code required to access a packed structure is usually slower and lengthier than the code required to access an equivalent nonpacked structure. Individual elements of packed structures cannot be passed as parameters to procedures and functions, hence cannot be used in calls to standard I/O routines.

In a packed structure which has another structure as a component (for example, a packed array of records), the component structures are not themselves packed unless explicitly specified by another occurrence of the keyword PACKED. Packed structures are considered to be of a different type than the equivalent nonpacked structures.

Pascal implementations typically have one or two additional predefined types. The most common are

```
TYPE
      TEXT: FILE OF CHAR;      (* usually available *)
      ALFA: PACKED ARRAY [1..n] OF CHAR;
(* in Pascal 8000, n = 8; on the CDC, n = 10 *)
```

UCSD Pascal also provides the types STRING[n], which is a string of n characters or fewer (where n cannot exceed 255), and "long integer," declared as INTEGER[n], where n is the maximum number of digits in the integer (up to a limit of 36). UCSD also provides the type TEXT, which is a PACKED FILE OF CHAR.

3.4 THE VAR SECTION

New variables are declared in the VAR section. The form of a declaration is

list_of_names : *type*

where the *list_of_names* consists of one or more simple names, separated by commas, and the *type* may be either the name or the description of a type.

```
VAR
      I, J: INTEGER;
      TODAY: DATE;       (* where DATE has been defined *)
      FLAG: BOOLEAN;     (*      in the TYPE section *)
      A, B: ARRAY [1..100] OF REAL;
      SCHEDULE: ARRAY [1..10] OF DATE;
```

In Pascal, storage space is allocated dynamically. This means that declarations are not descriptions of static entities determined once and for all at compile time, but rather are executable requests. Execution of a declaration in the VAR section consists of locating enough storage to hold a value of the designated type, and attaching the specified variable name to that storage. For example,

```
VAR
      A: ARRAY [1..10] OF INTEGER
```

actually creates the array and names it A.

Allocating space for variables does not include zeroing out of that space. The initial value of a variable is garbage, and it is the programmer's responsibility to assign it a value. When a variable is declared to be of a variant record type, enough space is allocated to hold the largest possible variant of that record.

Storage allocation is not permanent. When control leaves the procedure, function, or main program in which a VAR declaration occurs, the space used for those variables is taken away and recycled, and the variable names may no longer be used. For more details, see Section 7.3 on scope of names.

To ensure that two variables are of the same type, they should either be declared with the same type name, or they should occur in the sale *list of names* in the VAR section. Declaring two variables with the same type description does not always guarantee that they will have the same type (see Section 3.3 for more details).

3.5   THE VALUE SECTION (PASCAL 8000 ONLY)

Standard Pascal has no provision for initializing variables at compile time, as is done by the DATA statement of Fortran. Pascal 8000 provides a limited variable initialization capability in the VALUE section. A VALUE declaration has the form

variable := *constant*

where the variable has been declared in the VAR Section, and the constant is of the same type as the variable. The effect is to assign a value to the variable, just once, before execution of the program begins. The variable may be altered by the program (like any other variable), and the VALUE section will not have any further effect.

The VALUE section may only occur in the main program, since only there is it possible to allocate storage space to the variables at compile time.

Since Pascal 8000 provides set constants, array constants, and record constants (for records without variant parts), these may be used in the VALUE section.

There is little reason ever to use the VALUE section. It does not save any keypunching, and any time or storage space saved thereby is insignificant on an IBM 360/370. Since VALUE is not Standard Pascal, its use further degrades machine independence. Finally, whether you use it or not, VALUE is a reserved word which you may not use as a name in Pascal 8000, or in any program which you may someday want to run under Pascal 8000.

Chapter 4

EXPRESSIONS AND ASSIGNMENT STATEMENTS

One of Pascal's strongest points is the rich set of data types that it provides. Numbers are provided but, unlike many older languages, not everything must be represented in terms of numbers.

4.1 NUMERIC EXPRESSIONS

There are two kinds of numeric values in Standard Pascal, INTEGER and REAL. UCSD Pascal adds a third kind, INTEGER[n], for integers of up to n digits ($n <= 36$). An integer constant consists of one or more digits, optionally preceded by a sign ($+$ or $-$). It does not contain a decimal point.

Examples:

    5   −17   00025   +5836   0

On any given computer there is a limit to the size of integers. This limit is almost always over thirty thousand, and should not be a problem for most programs. If you want to know the limit on your system, there is a predefined identifier MAXINT which you may print out or otherwise use. (MAXINT is not a reserved word, so if you declare an identifier MAXINT of your own it overrides the predefined variable.)

On a one's complement machine, the smallest available integer is − MAXINT. On a machine which uses two's complement arithmetic the value will be given instead by − MAXINT − 1. You could not write this latter expression as − (MAXINT + 1) because that would cause arithmetic overflow. Care must be taken when working with such extreme values that not only the final result of a calculation but also all intermediate results be within the range − MAXINT to MAXINT.

In UCSD Pascal, integers and long integers can be freely intermixed in an expression, and the integers will be converted automatically to long integers. Any integer constant which exceeds MAXINT will be considered to be a long integer constant. You may assign an integer value to a long integer variable, but in order to assign a long integer value to an integer variable you must first ensure it is a legal integer value, then call TRUNC (*longinteger*) to convert it.

The arithmetic operations +, −, *, and DIV can be used with long integer values, as well as the comparison operators, but MOD cannot be used with long integers. Real numbers and long integers are incompatible— never mix them.

Real constants can be in either standard or scientific notation. A number in standard notation consists of one or more digits on both sides of a decimal point, optionally preceded by a sign (+ or −).

Examples:

    0.01   5.25   − 20.0   0.0   + 4500.00

Note that numbers with a decimal point at one end such as 3. or .5 are illegal within the program, although they may be used as input data. As far as I know, no justification for this restriction has ever been given. Numbers may not contain commas, spaces, or other extraneous characters.

Although it has an integral value, a number such as 5.00 is written as a real number, stored as a real number, and is considered to be a real number. The fact that its value happens to be integral is of no consequence.

Numbers can be written in scientific notation by suffixing either an integer or a standard real with an E followed by an optionally signed integer. The E is read as "times ten to the."

Examples:

    6.023E23   6023E20   3.1416E0
    1E6   − 1.0E − 10 6.626E − 27

The number following the E indicates the power of ten by which the number preceding the E is to be multiplied. Thus,

    93E6 = 93.0 * (10 ** 6) = 93000000.0

If you are not already familiar with scientific notation, an easy way to think of it is that the number following the E indicates the number of places to the right that the decimal point must be moved. A negative move to the right means, of course, that the move is actually to the left.

Real numbers span an enormous, but still limited, range. There is no predefined variable like MAXINT to help you determine this range, but it is usually at least $-1E38$ to $1E38$. If you need a clear idea of the limits on your machine, the following program should help.

```
PROGRAM REALRANGE(OUTPUT);
(* Determine approximate range of real numbers. *)
VAR
      X: REAL;
BEGIN
      X:=1.0;
      REPEAT
            X:=X+X;
            WRITELN(' ',X)
      UNTIL FALSE            (* actually, until overflow occurs *)
END.
```

Integers are stored on the computer with perfect accuracy. Real numbers are stored as approximate values, and should always be treated as such. Even those numbers which may be represented exactly in decimal, for example, 0.1, may not have an exact representation in binary. Hence, on most machines, the following is an infinite loop.

```
X:=0;
WHILE X <> 1.0 DO X:=X+0.1;        (* infinite loop *)
```

As a rule, you should never compare real numbers with the operators $=$ or $<>$, but only with $>$, $>=$, $<$, and $<=$.

If you are concerned with accuracy, a convenient number to know is the smallest number which can be added to 1.0 and still give a result different from 1.0.

```
PROGRAM FINDDELTA(OUTPUT);
(* Test accuracy of real numbers. *)
VAR
      SMALLREAL: REAL;
BEGIN
      SMALLREAL:=1/2;                        (* use 1/2, not 0.5 *)
      WHILE 1.0+SMALLREAL <> 1.0 DO          (* note use of <> *)
            SMALLREAL:=SMALLREAL/2;
      WRITELN (' SMALL REAL =', 2*SMALLREAL)
END.
```

Expressions may contain a mixture of integers and reals. The following operations are provided.

Symbol	Meaning	Result Type
+	add	If both operands are integer, the result is integer; if either or both operands are real, the result is real.
−	subtract	
*	multiply	
/	divide	The result is always real; no truncation occurs. Hence, 3/4 = 0.75, not 0.
DIV	Integer divide	Defined for integer operands only. The result is obtained by dividing the first operand by the second, and truncating the result toward zero.
MOD	Modulus, that is, remainder	Defined for integer operands only. The result is the remainder obtained when the first operand is divided by the second. If the result is nonzero, it has the sign of the first operand.

The last two operators are related by the equality

$$I = J*(I \text{ DIV } J) + (I \text{ MOD } J)$$

for I, J integer.

Standard Pascal does not support exponentiation. In Pascal 8000 exponentiation is denoted by **; for example, X**3 is X cubed. The result is integer if both operands are integer, and real otherwise.

To raise a positive value V to a real power X in standard Pascal, use EXP(X*LN(V)). (The EXP and LN functions are described below.) Note that it is mathematically meaningless to raise a negative number to a real power, in the same way that it is meaningless to divide by zero.

To raise a real variable V to an integer power I in Standard Pascal, use the following code.

```
FUNCTION POWER (V: REAL; I: INTEGER); REAL;
    (* Compute V**I *)
    VAR
        NEGATIVEEXPONENT: BOOLEAN;
        RESULT: REAL;
    BEGIN
        NEGATIVEEXPONENT:=(I < 0);
        I:=ABS(I);
        RESULT:=1;
        WHILE I > 0 DO
            IF ODD(I) THEN
                BEGIN
```

```
            RESULT: = V*RESULT;
            I: = I - 1
          END
        ELSE (* I is even *)
          BEGIN
            V: = V*V;
            I: = I DIV 2
          END;
        IF NEGATIVEEXPONENT THEN POWER: = 1/RESULT
        ELSE POWER: = RESULT
  END;
```

To raise an integer variable V to an integer power I, use the preceding code with V, RESULT, and POWER declared INTEGER rather than REAL.

It is legal to compare two reals, two integers, or a real and an integer (in either order) with the operators $<$, $<=$, $>$, $>=$, $=$, and $<>$. As previously noted, $=$ and $<>$ should be used with extreme care when real numbers are involved.

The following numeric functions are commonly available; your particular Pascal probably supplies additional functions not on this list. In all cases, the input parameter may be either REAL or INTEGER.

Function	Type of Result	Meaning
ABS(X)	Same as X.	Absolute value of X.
SQR(X)	Same as X.	Square of X, that is, X*X.
SQRT(X)	REAL	Square root of X.
SIN(X)	REAL	Sine of X (X in radians).
COS(X)	REAL	Cosine of X (X in radians).
ARCTAN(X)	REAL	Arctangent of X (X in radians). (This is named ATAN in UCSD Pascal.)
LN(X)	REAL	Natural logarithm (base e) of X.
EXP(X)	REAL	Exponential of X, that is, $e**X$.

Other common functions may be readily computed from the above.

```
LOG10(X)  =  LN(X)/LN(10)     Logarithm, base 10.
TAN(X)  =  SIN(X)/COS(X)      Tangent of X.
```

4.2 BOOLEAN EXPRESSIONS AND COMPARISONS

Boolean values and expressions are more important in Pascal than in many other languages because they are used extensively to control loops and IF statements. There are two Boolean constants: TRUE and FALSE.

Boolean values can arise in a number of ways: from comparisons ($=$, $<>$, $>$, $>=$, $<$, $<=$); from set membership tests (X IN S): or from calling a Boolean-valued function such as ODD(I), which returns TRUE if its integer parameter is odd and FALSE otherwise.

Three standard operators, AND, OR, and NOT, are defined for Boolean operands. NOT is a unary operator. AND and OR are binary.

NOT x is FALSE when x is TRUE, and TRUE when x is FALSE.

x AND y is TRUE when both x and y are TRUE, and FALSE when either or both of x and y are FALSE.

x OR y is TRUE when either or both of x and y are TRUE, and FALSE only when x and y are both FALSE.

The function ORD can be applied to Booleans, with ORD(FALSE) $= 0$ and ORD(TRUE) $= 1$. Consequently, comparisons are also defined on Booleans, with FALSE $<$ TRUE.

The following table relates the comparison operators to their usual names in formal logic. In each case, the meaning follows directly from the relationship FALSE $<$ TRUE.

$p = q$ p is equivalent to q

$p <> q$ p exclusive or q

$p <= q$ p implies q

$p >= q$ p is implied by q

$p > q$ p and not q

$p < q$ q and not p

Caution: Some logicians use the visually similar notation "P $\Leftarrow$ Q" to mean "Q implies P," but in Pascal "P $<=$ Q" computes as the reverse relation, "P implies Q."

It is probably best to use only AND, OR, NOT, $=$, and $<>$, since the meaning of these is clear even without knowing that FALSE $<$ TRUE in Pascal.

Comparisons may also be performed on operands which are integer, real, characters, strings, user-defined scalars, subranges, and (except for $<$ and $>$) sets. The result is always Boolean.

The following is illegal

```
1 <= X <= 10      (* illegal *)
```

because $1 <= X$ results in a Boolean value of TRUE or FALSE, which cannot then be compared with 10. The proper form is

```
(1 <= X)  AND  (X <= 10)
```

Because of Pascal's unusual order of precedence (see Section 4.4), it is best always to use parentheses when performing comparisons.

Comparisons with the constants TRUE and FALSE are almost always redundant and should be eliminated. For instance,

```
IF FLAG  =  TRUE THEN X: = X + 1
```

should be

```
IF FLAG THEN X: = X + 1
```

Similarly,

```
IF X  =  FALSE THEN X: = X – 1
```

should be rewritten as

```
IF NOT X THEN X: = X – 1
```

Finally, the roundabout construction

```
IF condition THEN FLAG: = TRUE
             ELSE FLAG: = FALSE
```

should always be replaced by the direct assignment

```
FLAG: = condition
```

Boolean values may be output (except in UCSD Pascal), but may not be input.

4.3 EXPRESSIONS INVOLVING OTHER DATA TYPES

A few operations are defined on data types other than REAL, INTEGER, and BOOLEAN. The comparison operators may be used on certain other types, as shown below. In all cases, the result is of type BOOLEAN.

=	<>	CHARs, strings, user-defined scalars, sets, and pointers
> =	< =	CHARs, strings, user-defined scalars, and sets
>	<	CHARs, strings, and user-defined scalars

The following operators are defined on sets and return a set as value.

+	set union
*	set intersection
–	set difference

Finally, x IN s yields the value TRUE if x occurs as a member of set s, and FALSE otherwise.

4.4   PRECEDENCE OF OPERATORS

The operations within an expression are performed in a particular order, depending on their position within the expression and their level of precedence. For example, both of the expressions

    2 + 3 * 4   and   3 * 4 + 2

evaluate to 14, because multiplication has a higher precedence than addition, and will be done first.

Two operators of equal precedence (such as + and −) will be done in a left-to-right order. Hence,

    10 − 5 + 2

evaluates as $(10 - 5) + 2 = 7$, not as $10 - (5 + 2) = 3$. The one exception to left-to-right evaluation is exponentiation in Pascal 8000, which is evaluated right-to-left: hence 4 ** 3 ** 2 is equivalent to 4 ** (3 ** 2).

Operators are grouped into five precedence levels, as follows.

(highest)   NOT

             **   (Pascal 8000)

             *, /, DIV, MOD, AND

             +, −, OR

(lowest)   =, <>, <, <=, >, >=, IN

Parentheses may always be used to specify the order of operations: the quantity within parentheses is computed first. For example, $(2 + 3) * 4 = 20$, not 14. It is perfectly legal to use parentheses even where they are not needed, to make the order of evaluation clear and explicit.

The precedence of operators is essentially the same as is used in algebra and in most other programming languages, so it should cause few problems. The one exception to this is the ill-chosen precedence of the logical operators AND, OR, and NOT, so that, for example,

    X < 10 AND Y < 10

has the implicit parenthesization

    (X < (10 AND Y)) < 10

which is of course illegal. You should write instead

    (X < 10) AND (Y < 10).

The relative precedence of the operators among themselves—first NOT, then AND, then OR—is standard and natural. Their precedence relative to other operators is not.

Rule: Whenever you mix a Boolean operator (NOT, AND, OR) with a comparison operator, use parentheses to make the order of evaluation explicit. Consistent application of this rule will not only make your program easier to read but can also protect you from some very hard-to-find bugs.

4.5   ASSIGNMENT STATEMENTS

An assignment statement has the form

variable := *expression*

where the *expression* may be as simple or as complex as desired, as long as it results in a value of exactly the same type as the *variable*. (See Section 3.3 on type equivalence.)

There are four exceptions to this rule.

1 File types may not be assigned.

2 An integer *expression* may be assigned to a real *variable*. The result will automatically be converted to a real number before assignment to the real variable. Similarly, in UCSD Pascal an integer *expression* may be assigned to a long integer *variable*.

3 A set *expression* may be assigned to a set *variable* if (a) the sets are either both packed or both nonpacked, and (b) the elements of the sets are of the same or compatible types.

4 If either the *variable* or the *expression* (or both) is a subrange of some type, that type will be used in the test for type equivalence. For example, if

```
VAR
    I: 1..10;
    J: INTEGER;
```

then

```
I:=J
```

is syntactically correct, and will compile correctly. However, runtime tests will usually be inserted, so that if J is not in the range 1..10 when the assignment statement is attempted, a runtime error will result.

The statement

```
J:=I
```

is also syntactically correct, but no runtime checking need be done.

It follows that arrays may be assigned to array variables (if they are of the same type), records may be assigned to record variables (if they are of the same type), sets may be assigned to set variables (if they are of the same type), and so on. For example, given the declarations

```
VAR
     R: RECORD
              X, Y: REAL
          END;
     S: PACKED ARRAY [1..5] OF CHAR;
     T: SET OF 1..20;
     U: ARRAY [1..3] OF INTEGER;
```

the following assignments are legal.

```
R: = (# 1.0, 1.0 #);        (* Pascal 8000 only *)
S: = 'HELLO';
T: = [1, 3, 5, 7];
U: = (# 0, 0, 0 #);         (* Pascal 8000 only *)
```

The string 'HELLO' is of type PACKED ARRAY [1..5] OF CHAR, hence may be assigned to S. The string 'HI' could not be assigned to S, however, as it is of the wrong type. 'HI' is of type PACKED ARRAY [1..2] OF CHAR. T is of type SET OF 1..20, where 1..20 is a subrange of IN-TEGER, hence assignment of the set [1, 3, 5, 7] to T is legal. The assign-ments to R and U are legal only in Pascal 8000, because Standard Pascal does not have record and array constants.

Note that Pascal does not allow assignment of a real value to an integer variable. For example, the following is illegal.

```
VAR
     PI: INTEGER;
. . .
PI: = 3.1416;              (* illegal *)
```

This is done to protect you from inadvertently losing the fractional part of the number. You may do the assignment only if you explicitly round or truncate:

```
PI: = ROUND(3.1416)
```

or

```
PI: = TRUNC(3.1416)
```

Finally, Pascal 8000 provides a "type-change" operation, by which you can consider an expression to be of any desired type. You do this by using the name of the desired type as if it were a one-parameter function, for example,

```
PI: = INTEGER(3.1416)
```

assigns PI (part of) the value 3.1416.

It is important to realize that no type conversion is done. Hence, the value of INTEGER (3.1416) is actually a real number masquerading as an integer. On the IBM 360/370, real numbers occupy more storage than integers, so the value assigned to PI is actually only the first half of the real number 3.1416.

In other versions of Pascal it is often possible to use a variant record to implement your own type-change functions (see Section 12.4 for details).

Pascal goes to considerable effort to protect the user from accidentally using data of the wrong type. Type-change functions specifically permit any type of data to masquerade as any other type, thus circumventing Pascal's type checking. Accordingly, type-change functions should be avoided unless the need is very clear.

Chapter 5

CONDITIONAL STATEMENTS

It is often necessary to take one of several different actions, depending on circumstances. Pascal provides three constructs for doing this: (1) the IF–THEN statement, which determines whether or not to perform a single action; (2) the IF–THEN–ELSE statement, which determines which of two alternative actions to perform; (3) the CASE statement, which determines which of many alternative actions to perform.

The IF–THEN and IF–THEN–ELSE statements are usually considered to be two variations of the IF statement and will be discussed together in Section 5.1. The CASE statement is discussed in Section 5.2, along with a similar structure built from IF statements, the IF . . . ELSE IF . . . ELSE IF . . . ELSE statement.

5.1 THE IF STATEMENT

The first variety of IF statement has the form

   IF *condition* THEN *statement*

where *condition* is any expression which results in a Boolean value, and *statement* is any single statement. To execute the IF statement, the *condition* is first evaluated and, if it is TRUE, the *statement* is executed. If the *condition* is FALSE, the IF statement does nothing. In either case, control then passes to the next statement.

The IF–THEN statement (without ELSE) is used primarily as a glitch remover, to repair irregularities in the data. That is, it can usually be considered to have the meaning

IF *something is wrong* THEN *fix it*

For example, the following statement ensures that there is room on the current output line for the next item (where there may be as many as NUMPERLINE items per line) by advancing to the next line if the current line is full.

```
IF NOWONLINE > = NUMPERLINE THEN      (* if out of room *)
    BEGIN
    WRITELN;
    NOWONLINE: = 0
    END;
(* Now there is enough room, whether or not there was before. *)
```

The other variety of IF statement has the form

IF *condition* THEN *statement_1* ELSE *statement_2*

The *condition* is evaluated and, if TRUE, *statement_1* is executed; but if FALSE, *statement_2* is executed. Whichever one is executed, control then passes to the statement following the IF–THEN–ELSE.

For example,

```
IF X > Y THEN MAX: = X ELSE MAX: = Y

IF SCORE[I] > = 0 THEN VALID: = VALID + 1
                  ELSE INVALID: = INVALID + 1

IF A[I] > A[I + 1] THEN
    BEGIN
    TEMP: = A[I]; A[I]: = A[I + 1]; A[I + 1]: = TEMP;
    I: = I − 1
    END
ELSE
    I: = I + 1
```

Usually both statements under control of the IF–THEN–ELSE are intended to produce the same final result, although by different methods. In the examples above, MAX is set to the larger value; the number of valid and invalid scores are counted; and (as part of a bubble sort) array A becomes slightly more sorted, while index I is set to the next array location to be checked.

Recall that semicolons are used to separate statements. As a result, the following construction is illegal.

IF *condition* THEN *statement_1*; ELSE *statement_2*   (* illegal *)

The extra semicolon changes this from the intended IF–THEN–ELSE statement to an IF–THEN statement followed by an ELSE statement. Since there is no such thing as an ELSE statement, the compiler will give an error message.

IF statements may be nested, that is, the statement or statements under control of an IF statement may themselves be IF statements.

```
IF COST > 10.00 THEN
    IF COST <= 50.00 THEN WRITECHECK
    ELSE CHARGEIT
ELSE  (* COST <= 10.00 *)
      PAYCASH
```

A minor ambiguity can arise when IF statements are nested.

```
IF condition_1 THEN IF condition_2
   THEN statement_1 ELSE statement_2
```

It is not clear with which IF the ELSE is associated. Is *statement_2* executed when *condition_1* is FALSE, or when *condition_1* is TRUE and *condition_2* FALSE? This ambiguity is called the "dangling ELSE" problem, and in Pascal it is always resolved by associating the ELSE with the nearest preceding IF which does not already have an associated ELSE. Thus the above construct is equivalent to

```
IF condition_1 THEN
    BEGIN
    IF condition_2 THEN statement_1 ELSE statement_2
    END
```

If you wish to associate the ELSE with the first IF, you do this by inserting an explicit BEGIN and END.

```
IF condition_1 THEN
    BEGIN
    IF condition_2 THEN statement_1
    END
ELSE statement_2
```

Indentation which shows how IF statements are nested can make the program considerably easier to read. However, if the indentation does not match the actual nesting, as in

```
IF condition_1 THEN         (* dangerous indentation *)
    IF condition_2 THEN statement_1
ELSE statement 2
```

the result may be a bug which is well camouflaged and very hard to find. Indentation is important, and should be done with care.

When dealing with any but the simplest IF statements, it is good practice to put a comment after the ELSE giving the negation of the IF condition. This is especially helpful with deeply nested IF statements.

```
IF (I < ARRAYSIZE) AND (NOT FOUND) THEN
    BEGIN
    I: = I + 1;
    FOUND: = (A[I] = KEY)
    END
ELSE (* (I > = ARRAYSIZE) OR FOUND *)
    . . .
```

When the condition of the IF statement is complex, it is better to work out the proper negation (as above), rather than to just slap a NOT in front of it. In the above example, the comment

```
ELSE (* NOT((I < ARRAYSIZE) AND (NOT FOUND)) *)
```

would not be so helpful. It is not much extra work to do this, because you have to know what the negation is in order to get the ELSE part right anyway. You might as well do it just once and write it down.

Of course, it is best to keep your tests simple. Since this is not always possible, you should know the following three rules for figuring out the negation of a condition.

1 NOT (NOT X)   = X

2 NOT (X AND Y) = (NOT X) OR (NOT Y)

3 NOT (X OR Y)   = (NOT X) AND (NOT Y)

5.2   THE CASE STATEMENT

The CASE statement is used to select one statement for execution from among several alternatives. Its form is

```
CASE expression OF
        list_of_values_1: statement_1;
        list_of_values_2: statement_2;
        . . .
        list_of_values_N: statement_N      (* no ";" *)
    END
```

where each *list_of_values* consists of one or more constants of the same type as the *expression*. This type must be one of the following: INTEGER, CHAR, BOOLEAN, enumeration, or subrange. No constant may occur more than once within the CASE statement.

The *expression* is evaluated, and the resultant value is searched for and found in some *list_of_values*, then the *statement* associated with that list is executed, and control passes to the next statement following the CASE. If the value computed by the *expression* does not occur in any *list_of_values*, the operation of the CASE statement is undefined (and may be catastrophic). If you are lucky, you will get a runtime error message; if you are not, the result with be a mysterious bug. UCSD Pascal specifically defines the CASE statement to do nothing if the value is not found.

Example of a CASE statement:

```
CASE MONTHNUMBER OF
      4, 6, 9, 11: DAYS:=30;
      1, 3, 5, 7, 8, 10, 12: DAYS:=31;
      2: IF LEAPYEAR THEN DAYS:=29 ELSE DAYS:=28
END
```

To protect yourself against unexpected month numbers, you can use an IF statement as a guard for the CASE statement.

```
IF   (MONTHNUMBER >= 1) AND (MONTHNUMBER <= 12) THEN
      CASE MONTHNUMBER OF
            . . .
      END
ELSE
      WRITELN (' *ERROR* ILLEGAL MONTH: ', MONTHNUMBER)
```

Some versions of Pascal provide a default value ELSE (Pascal 8000) or OTHERS (PASLC) that can be used in this situation.

```
CASE MONTHNUMBER OF
      4, 6, 9, 11: DAYS:=30;
      1, 3, 5, 7, 8, 10, 12: DAYS:=31;
      2: IF LEAPYEAR THEN DAYS:=29 ELSE DAYS:=28;
      ELSE: WRITELN (' *ERROR* ILLEGAL MONTH: ', MONTHNUMBER)
END
```

There can be at most one ELSE: (or OTHERS:) in a CASE statement, and it should always occur by itself as the last case before the END.

Pascal 8000 also allows subrange notation in a *list_of_values*.

```
CASE GRADE OF
      90..100: LETTER:= 'A';
      80..89:  LETTER:= 'B';
      70..79:  LETTER:= 'C';
      60..69:  LETTER:= 'D';
      0..59:   LETTER:= 'F';
      ELSE:  WRITELN(' *ERROR* INVALID GRADE: ', GRADE)
END
```

Sometimes the CASE statement is not powerful enough, either because the conditions are more complex than mere lists of values, or because the values are not simple types (for example, they may be strings).

The IF statement may be nested in such a way as to simulate a more powerful CASE statement. This is done by testing for the first remaining situation in the IF part, and using successive ELSE IFs to test the remaining cases; a final ELSE can be used either to process the last case, or to process illegal values if all legal cases have been covered above.

```
(* Find roots of a quadratic equation a*x**2 + b*x + c *)
DISCRIMINANT: = B*B − 4*A*C;
IF DISCRIMINANT > 0 THEN
    BEGIN
    TEMP: = SQRT(DISCRIMINANT);
    ROOT1: = ( − B + TEMP)/(A + A);
    ROOT2: = ( − B − TEMP)/(A + A);
    REALROOTS: = 2
    END
ELSE  IF DISCRIMINANT = 0 THEN
    BEGIN
    ROOT1: = − B/(A + A);
    ROOT2: = ROOT1;
    REALROOTS: = 1
    END
ELSE (* DISCRIMINANT < 0 *)
    REALROOTS: = 0
```

Chapter 6

LOOPS

There are three kinds of loop in Pascal: WHILE, REPEAT, and FOR. PASLC adds a fourth kind, LOOP, while Pascal 8000 adds a fourth, LOOP, and a fifth, FORALL. The two (different) LOOP statements are general purpose loops, and are discussed in this chapter. The FORALL loop is used only with sets, and is discussed in Section 13.2. Since you already know something about loops from Chapter 1, we begin with a discussion of when each type is appropriate.

6.1 WHEN TO USE EACH KIND OF LOOP

The WHILE loop is the simplest kind of loop, and should be used whenever there is no clear reason for using one of the other loops. A WHILE loop executes while a given condition holds and stops when it no longer holds. Since the test is at the top of the loop, the loop may execute zero times, that is, not at all. This means there is never a need for an explicit test to bypass the loop.

For example, to find the first nonzero value in an array (if there is one), you may write

```
I := 1;
WHILE (A[I]) = 0) AND (I < ARYSIZE) DO I := I+1
```

The REPEAT loop has its test at the bottom of the loop, so that the loop body always gets executed at least once. This form of loop should be used when the exit test is logically meaningless unless the loop body has been executed, for example, if the computation has the form

```
REPEAT try something UNTIL successful
```

If you find youself writing code to bypass a REPEAT loop, for example,

```
IF NOT (condition) THEN
    REPEAT something UNTIL condition
```

you should use the simpler but equivalent form

```
WHILE NOT (condition) DO something
```

Another situation that sometimes arises is that it is necessary to bypass, not the entire REPEAT loop body, but only the last portion of it, as follows.

```
REPEAT
    some_statements;
    DONE := condition;
    IF NOT DONE THEN
        BEGIN
        more_statements
        END
UNTIL DONE
```

If the code for *some_statements* is short, it is often better to duplicate this code and use a WHILE loop.

```
some_statements;
WHILE NOT (condition) DO
    BEGIN
    more_statements;
    some_statements
    END
```

The FOR loop is more complex than either of the above loops because it is not a pure loop: it also manipulates data (the loop index). Readers who doubt that this fact adds much complexity should glance at the discussion of FOR loops in this chapter.

A FOR loop should be used only when the exact number of iterations is known in advance. Most of the time this means when every element of an array needs to be processed; stepping through arrays is the primary use of FOR loops. If there is any possibility that not all array elements need be processed, some other kind of loop should be used. FOR loops tend to be badly overused by programmers who already know a language (for example, Fortran IV) in which this is the only kind of loop available.

Just as the FOR loop is used to process all the elements of an array, the FORALL loop (Pascal 8000 only) is used to process all the elements of a set.

Pascal 8000 also provides a loop with multiple exits, called LOOP. LOOP is a powerful and flexible control structure; too powerful, in fact, because it can easily be used where a simpler form of loop would suffice, thus making it easier to write a less readable program. While there are legitimate uses for the LOOP statement, it should not be used until the alternatives have been thoroughly explored.

6.2   THE WHILE LOOP

The syntax of the WHILE loop is

WHILE *condition* DO *statement*

where the *condition* may be any expression resulting in a Boolean value, and the *statement* is often a compound statement (BEGIN *statements* END). The loop operates as follows. The *condition* is evaluated; if FALSE, the loop exits. Otherwise, the *statement* is executed, and control returns to the top of the loop, to test the *condition* again. Clearly, the *statement* is only executed when the *condition* is TRUE; when (and if) the WHILE loop exits, the *condition* has been made FALSE.

6.3   THE REPEAT LOOP

The syntax of a REPEAT loop is

REPEAT *sequence_of_statements* UNTIL *condition*

where the *sequence_of_statements* may be one or more statements. BEGIN and END are not required because the keywords REPEAT and UNTIL serve as brackets. The *condition* may be any expression which results in a Boolean value.

Operation is as follows. The *sequence_of_statements* is executed, then the *condition* is evaluated; if the *condition* is TRUE the loop exits, but if it is FALSE control returns to the top of the loop, to execute the *sequence_of_statements* again. Clearly, the *condition* will be TRUE when (and if) the REPEAT loop exits.

Caution: Do not assume that the *sequence_of_statements* is only executed with the *condition* FALSE. The loop test is at the bottom, so the first time through the loop body the *condition* is untested, and may be TRUE (or even undefined). Special attention must be given to ensure that the *sequence_of_statements* works properly the first time through the loop.

6.4   THE FOR LOOP

The syntax of the FOR loop is

FOR *index* := *initial_value* TO *final_value* DO *statement* where

> *index* is a simple unsubscripted variable of type INTEGER, CHAR, BOOLEAN, subrange, or enumeraton.
>
> *initial_value* and *final_value* are expressions that result in values of a type that may be assigned to the *index*.
>
> *statement* is a single statement that obeys the constraints given below.

The operation of the FOR loop is approximately as follows.

```
TEMP1 := initial_value;
TEMP2 := final_value;
IF TEMP1 <= TEMP2 THEN
    BEGIN
    index := TEMP1;
    statement;
    WHILE index <> TEMP2 DO
        BEGIN
        index := SUCC (index);
        statement
        END
    END
END
```

Hence the *statement* which forms the loop body is executed once for each value of the index from the *initial_value* through the *final_value*, inclusive. If the given *initial_value* is equal to the *final_value*, the loop body is executed once; if larger, the loop body is not executed at all.

SUCC is used to step from one value of *index* to the next. SUCC can be applied to integers, characters, Booleans, enumerations, or subranges of these, that is, any legal index. The SUCCessor of an integer is simply that integer plus one.

The complexity of the above WHILE loop and the need to write the *statement* twice arise because it may be illegal to compute values outside of the range covered by the FOR loop: the *final_value* may not have a SUCCessor.

The above description of the operation of a FOR loop is only approximate for the following reasons. First, Pascal does not allow the *statement* to do anything that would change the value of the *index*. This is to give the implementor freedom to produce efficient code. (If you want to alter the *index* either to get out of the loop early, or to stay in the loop longer, you should be using a WHILE or a REPEAT loop instead.)

Similarly, it is poor form (and possibly illegal on some compilers) for the statement to alter the *initial_value* or the *final_value*. According to the above description, in terms of a WHILE loop, this should not affect the number of times that the loop is executed, but you cannot depend on that.

Second, upon final exit from the loop, the value of the *index* is undefined. This means that you cannot ever be sure what that value is; you can use the variable again, but be sure to assign it a value first.

In this context, "undefined" means that the person who implemented your Pascal compiler was free to do whatever he pleased—and it may not have been the same thing in every situation. Undefined is a red flag, indicating that the language definition is incomplete at that point. If you learn what your particular compiler does and use that knowledge, you are asking for trouble. Your programs will be more obscure, will not work on another Pascal system, and may not work on the next version of your own system. Moreover, your compiler may do different things in different contexts. Undefined is another word for poison.

To be safe, (1) you may use the values of the *index*, *initial_value*, and *final_value* within the loop but you should never modify them there, and (2) never expect the *index* to have a meaningful value once the loop terminates.

You cannot choose the amount by which the *index* is incremented; it is always the SUCCessor of the current value. However, it is possible to make the loop run backwards, each time taking the PREDecessor of the current index value rather than its SUCCessor. This is done by using the keyword DOWNTO in place of TO.

FOR *index* := *initial_value* DOWNTO *final_value* DO *statement*

The operation of the FOR...DOWNTO loop is closely analogous to the operation of the FOR...TO loop. Since the *index* counts down rather than up, the *initial_value* is generally greater than the *final_value*; if the *initial_value* is less than the *final_value*, the loop body in a FOR...DOWNTO loop is not executed at all.

6.5   THE LOOP STATEMENT (PASCAL 8000 ONLY)

There are two varieties of LOOP statement. One variety has a POSTLUDE part and the other does not. These varieties will be considered separately.

The LOOP without a POSTLUDE has the form

LOOP *sequence_of_statements* END

where the *sequence_of_statements* consists of one or more statements. BEGIN is not needed because the statements are bracketed by the keywords LOOP and END.

The semantics is trivial. The *sequence_of_statements* is executed an indefinite number of times. By itself, the LOOP...END construct is an infinite loop.

To escape the loop, an EXIT is used. EXIT looks and acts like a statement, except that it can only be used within a LOOP...END. The syntax is simply

    EXIT

and the semantics is that execution of the (one) immediately enclosing LOOP...END is terminated and control passes to the following statement, if any. EXIT terminates only the innermost LOOP in which it occurs. It cannot be used to exit multiple nested LOOPs.

Typically, an EXIT is used in one of the alternatives of an IF or CASE statement to provide conditional loop termination. As many EXIT statements as desired may be used within a LOOP...END.

Use of multiple exits leads to a problem. When the loop does exit, it is often desirable to know why, that is, which EXIT was taken. To provide this information, the undifferentiated EXIT may be replaced by a number of distinguishable exit signals, called "events;" the syntax is rather complex.

    LOOP UNTIL *list_of_events* :   (* colon, not semicolon *)
            sequence_of_statements   (* no semicolon *)
    POSTLUDE
            event : *statement* ;
            event : *statement* ;
            . . .
            event : *statement*   (* no semicolon *)
    END

where

An *event* is an identifier; the scope of the identifier is the LOOP statement in which it occurs.

The *list_of_events* consists of one or more event names, separated by commas.

The *sequence_of_statements* constitute the loop body, that is, the part which is executed repeatedly.

The event names are declared by their appearance in the *list_of_events*; they need and should have no other declaration.

The event names are used inside the loop body as if they were statements. Execution of an *event* causes the loop body to terminate immediately. Control then passes to the POSTLUDE, which acts like a CASE statement with the *event* as a selector, that is, the *statement* in the POSTLUDE labeled with the appropriate *event* is executed, and control then passes to the statement (if any) following the END.

EXIT is not a true statement, but rather a predefined event name. EXIT may also be used in a LOOP with a POSTLUDE (it is not declared in the *list_of_events*). When used, it means that no POSTLUDE action should be taken, but rather that control should pass immediately to the statement (if any) following the END. Hence EXIT should not be used as a label in the POSTLUDE.

As an example, the following code searches an array *A* for a given KEY, and inserts it if it is not already present.

```
I:=1;
LOOP UNTIL FOUND, ABSENT, OVERFLOW:
        IF A[I] = KEY THEN FOUND;
        I:=I+1;
        IF I > ARYSIZE THEN OVERFLOW;
        IF I > NUMBEROFENTRIES THEN ABSENT
POSTLUDE
        FOUND: WRITELN(' FOUND ', KEY, ' AT LOCATION ', I);
        OVERFLOW: WRITELN(' ***** TABLE CAPACITY EXCEEDED. ');
        ABSENT:
            BEGIN
                NUMBEROFENTRIES:=I;
                A[I]:=KEY;
                WRITELN(' ', KEY, ' INSERTED AT LOCATION ', I)
            END
END
```

6.6   THE LOOP STATEMENT (PASLC ONLY)

Some, but possibly not all, implementations of PASLC on the DEC-10 have a LOOP statement which superficially resembles the simple form of the Pascal 8000 LOOP statement, but it is not the same. The form is

```
LOOP
        sequence_of_statements_1        (* no semicolon *)
    EXIT  IF condition;
        sequence_of_statements_2        (* no semicolon *)
END
```

This is a loop with a test in the middle, sometimes called an N-and-a-half loop. The EXIT IF occurs exactly once, and causes the loop to exit when the condition becomes true at that point. Since either *sequence_of_statements* may be empty, the LOOP can easily be used to simulate either a WHILE loop or a REPEAT loop.

LOOP can sometimes be handy, but it is nonstandard, so should be avoided if there is any chance of moving the program to another machine in the future.

Chapter 7

PROCEDURES AND FUNCTIONS

There are two types of subprograms in Pascal: procedures and functions. Generally speaking, a procedure is used to perform an action, while a function is used to compute a value. We use the name "routine" to mean either a procedure or a function.

7.1 SYNTAX OF PROCEDURES AND FUNCTIONS

Routines are declared within a program, as are variables and constants. The form of a procedure declaration is

```
PROCEDURE procedure_name formal_parameter_list ;
     declarations;
     BEGIN
     sequence_of_statements
     END
```

while the form of a function declaration is

```
FUNCTION function_name formal_parameter_list : result type ;
     declarations;
     BEGIN
     sequence_of_statements
     END
```

The *procedure_name* and the *function_name* may be any identifiers.

These names are used later to call the routine.

The *formal_parameter_list* is a list of variables and their types. It is omitted if no parameters are needed. When there is a formal parameter list, it has the following form.

(*mode list_of_identifiers* : *type_name* ;

   . . .

   mode list_of_identifiers : *type_name*)

This takes some explanation.

The *list_of_identifiers* is just a list of (one or more) names that will be used as variables in the routine. When the list includes more than one identifier, the identifiers are separated by commas. The *type_name* tells the type of those identifiers. It must be a NAME, not a description (for example, AR-RAY[1..10] OF INTEGER is illegal here), except for Pascal 8000, where it may be either.

Example:

   (X, Y: INTEGER; Z: REAL)

Here the first *list_of_identifiers* consists of X and Y, both integers, while the second *list_of_identifiers* consists of Z alone, which is a real. This could have been written with no change in meaning as

   (X: INTEGER; Y: INTEGER; Z: REAL)

The *mode* refers to the mode of parameter transmission. It can be either (1) omitted, as in the above examples, in which case parameters are transmitted by value, or (2) it can be the word VAR, in which case parameters are transmitted by reference. These modes are described in the next section. Note that the word VAR in a parameter list has an entirely different meaning from the word VAR as used to initiate the declaration of variables.

Declarations inside a routine may include any and all of the types of declarations available elsewhere (except VALUE in Pascal 8000). In particular, you may declare functions and procedures inside other functions and procedures. Likewise, statements inside a routine may include any and all of the types of statements available elsewhere.

To return a value from a function, you assign that value to the name of the function, just as though that name were a variable of the appropiate type. Do not be misled, however. The function name is NOT a variable and should not be treated as one.

The body of a function or procedure consists of a single compound statement (with BEGIN and END). Control returns to the calling program or routine when that statement is finished executing; there is no explicit RE-TURN statement. UCSD Pascal works the same way, but also has a procedure EXIT which acts somewhat like a RETURN statement in other languages. The form is

EXIT (*routine_name*)

or

EXIT (PROGRAM)

The *routine_name* may be the name of a function, procedure, or the main program. If the name is that of the routine in which the call to EXIT occurs, it does a normal return; if it is the name of another routine, all routines back to and including that routine will return. In the case of a recursive call, the most recent invocation of the named routine will return.

Exiting the main program, either by naming it in an EXIT call or by giving EXIT the reserved word PROGRAM, causes program termination.

EXIT is not commonly accepted in current structured programming practice, and should probably be avoided.

7.2 PARAMETER TRANSMISSION

When a routine is called, we normally want to give the routine some information and/or to get some information back. This can be done by parameter lists, by global variables, or by a combination of the two. (Functions also return a value as a result of the function call.) In this section we discuss only parameter lists.

When a routine is declared, it is declared with a (possibly empty) "formal parameter list." When the routine is called, it is called with an "actual parameter list." For example, if we declare,

PROCEDURE DOITNOW (I: INTEGER; CH: CHAR)

and then call this procedure with the statement

DOITNOW (N, '*')

then I and CH are the formal parameters, while N and '*' are the actual parameters. Formal parameters must always be simple identifiers, without any subscripts or other frills, but actual parameters may sometimes be constants or expressions, as we shall see shortly.

Parameters are paired: one actual parameter matches one formal parameter. In this example N is paired with I, while '*' is paired with CH. There must be exactly as many actual parameters in a routine call as there are formal parameters in the declaration of that routine, in order for this pairing to be possible. Pairing is done strictly by position: the first actual parameter is paired with the first formal parameter, the second actual with the second formal, and so on. Finally, the types of the paired parameters must match: I is declared INTEGER, so N must be an integer; CH is declared CHAR, so '*' must be (and is) a character. Once the pairing is done, information can be transmitted between the members of each pair: N and I can communicate, as can CH and '*'.

There are two modes of parameter transmission available in Pascal: "by value" and "by reference." Call by value is the default mode; you get it automatically unless you say VAR. VAR causes parameters to be called by reference. The current example, without VAR, uses call by value.

Call by value is a one-way street. It allows you to give information to the routine, but does not allow any information to come back to you. When DOITNOW is called, it is as if the following assignments were made just before DOITNOW begins execution.

```
I := N;
CH := '*'
```

(This is why the types had to match.) In this way DOITNOW is informed of the values of N and '*'. However, it has no way to return any information. Anything that DOITNOW does to I or CH will not affect N or '*' and when it returns, the variables I and CH will no longer exist, because of the scope rules (see the next section).

For call by value, the actual parameters may be variables, constants, or expressions, as long as they result in values which may legally be assigned to the corresponding formal parameters. In particular, an integer actual parameter may be paired with a real formal parameter, since Pascal specifically allows assignment of an integer value to a real variable (and automatically converts it to a real value during the assignment).

On some machines, variables are initialized by the compiler to a special value called <undefined>, and it is illegal to use such variables until they have been assigned values. On these machines it may therefore be illegal to pass such variables by value, so make certain they do have a value before the routine call. This is good practice in any case.

Call by reference is a two-way street. It allows you to pass information to and receive information from a routine. To get this mode, put VAR before a list of identifiers in the formal parameter list, and those identifiers (up to the next semicolon) will be called by reference. Fortran, incidentally, uses this mode exclusively.

In call by reference, the formal parameters do not really exist as independent variables; when the routine is called, their names become aliases for the actual parameters. Any values the actual parameters have, the formal parameters share. Any changes to the formal parameters are actually done to the actual parameters. This is why they are called "actual."

For example,

```
TYPE
     VECTOR = ARRAY[1..100] OF REAL;
VAR
     A: VECTOR;
. . .
PROCEDURE SORT (VAR V: VECTOR);
. . .
END (* SORT *);
. . .
SORT (A)
```

In this example there is actually only one vector, vector A. When SORT is called, V becomes an alias, or alternate name, for A. SORT can examine the contents of V (but it is really examining A), and it can change the values in V (but it is really changing the values in A). If it sorts vector V and returns, we find that vector A has been sorted.

One implication of call by reference is that the types of actual parameters must be identical to the types of the corresponding formal parameters, since a variable can be of only one type. Another implication is that the formal parameters cannot be constants or expressions—the routine may change their values, and it makes no sense to change the value of a constant or expression. Finally, since call by reference does not perform an implied assignment, it is legal to use a variable which has not yet been assigned a value as an actual parameter (provided, of course, that the routine does not attempt to use that underfined value).

There are two logical errors you can make with parameter lists. First, if you forget to declare a parameter VAR, your routine will appear to not do anything: your parameter values will be the same after the call as before. Second, if you declare a parameter VAR when you should not, your routine may change parameters you did not expect it to change.

The first of these is a clear error, and can be fixed. The second is an extra fact to remember about the routine, and as such is a threat which will hang over you for the lifetime of the routine, even if everything works right now. The moral is: unless it is the specific purpose of a procedure to change a given parameter, do not make it a VAR parameter.

Functions should not have VAR parameters, even though it is legal. Consider the following example.

```
FUNCTION BUMP (VAR X: INTEGER): INTEGER;
     BEGIN
     X := X+1;
     BUMP := 2*X
     END;
```

```
. . .
X := 1;
Y := X + BUMP(X)
```

Is Y assigned the value 5 or the value 6? It could be either, depending on whether the old or the new value of X was added to BUMP(X). Whichever your compiler does, it is folly to trust the result.

Despite the above admonitions against VAR parameters, there are some exceptions. Passing a parameter by value involves copying its value, and in the case of arrays and other large structures this can incur considerable overhead. If efficiency is a major concern, this overhead can be avoided by passing such parameters by reference (with VAR). You are under no obligation to modify parameters passed by reference, and in particular, functions should never modify any of their parameters.

In closing this section, we note some limitations of Pascal parameter transmission. Pascal expects parameters that are passed by reference to start at word (or byte) boundaries. Thus, if an array or record is declared PACKED, individual elements of that structure cannot be passed by reference. Entire PACKED structures can be passed as usual, however, and there are no restrictions on passing elements of a packed structure by value.

Because of the type restrictions on parameters, there is no way to pass arrays of varying sizes to routines. Thus, for example, you can write a routine SORT to sort an array of exactly 100 integers, but you cannot write one to sort an array of N integers. This is widely regarded as a major design flaw of Pascal, and sooner or later it will have to be fixed. (For a while it appeared that the new ANSI Standard for Pascal would introduce "conformant-array-schemas" to solve this problem, but this proposal was deleted again in the May 1981 version of the Standard.) In the meantime, see Section 3.3 for some hints on ways to get around the problem.

7.3   SCOPE OF NAMES

Names in Pascal may refer to any of a number of things. Constants, variables, procedures, and functions may all have names; so may new data types. A label is a kind of name, even though the name consists of digits only. Fields in a record have names, as do the possible values of a user-defined scalar type.

Names may be declared at the top of a Pascal program. They may also be declared within functions and procedures. The scope of a name is that part of the code in which the name may be used. Generally speaking, a name declared at the top of program may be used anywhere throughout the code; a name declared within a routine may be used anywhere the routine (including within any routines nested within that routine), but not outside the routine.

The only exception to this rule is when one name temporarily covers up a previous usage of the same name.

The same name may not be used for two distinct purposes within a single block of declarations. However, names may be declared inside a routine that are identical to names outside the routine. When this happens, the new name temporarily covers up the outside name. Any use of the name refers to the local declaration, that is, the one inside the routine. Outside the routine, the name refers to the outside declaration.

Names declared within a routine are said to be local to that routine; names inherited from outside the routine are said to be global. Current thinking is that the use of global variables should be minimized.

Figure 6.1 illustrates the essential points made above. A more complex example follows, in which the scope rules are applied to several different kinds of names (but the same principles apply).

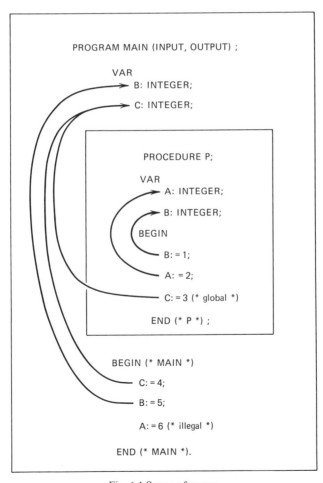

Fig. 6.1 Scope of names.

```
PROGRAM SCOPERULES (INPUT, OUTPUT);
   VAR
         I:      INTEGER;
         X:      REAL;
         CHOICE: (YES, NO, MAYBE);
   . . .
   PROCEDURE SIMPLE (K: INTEGER);
      VAR
            TEMP: INTEGER;
      PROCEDURE NESTED (Y: REAL);
            VAR Z: REAL;
            BEGIN
            (* Names available are I, X, CHOICE, YES, NO, MAYBE,
            SIMPLE, K, TEMP, NESTED, Y, and Z. *)
            END;
      BEGIN
      (* Names available are I, X, CHOICE, YES, NO, MAYBE,
      SIMPLE, K, NESTED, and TEMP. CONFLICT has not yet been
      defined, and is not available; Y and Z are no longer available. *)
      END;
   . . .
   FUNCTION CONFLICT (N, X: INTEGER): BOOLEAN;
      CONST
            PI = 3.1415926536;
            NO = 25;
      BEGIN
      (* Names available are I, CHOICE, YES, MAYBE, SIMPLE,
      CONFLICT, N, X, PI, and NO. K, TEMP, NESTED, Y, and Z are
      not available at all; the X that is available is the integer parameter,
      not the other one; and NO is a synonym for 25. *)
      END;
   . . .
   BEGIN (* MAIN PROGRAM *)
   (* Names available here are I,X (the REAL one), CHOICE, YES, NO (a
   scalar constant of type CHOICE), MAYBE, SIMPLE, and CONFLICT.
   The names K, TEMP, NESTED, Y, Z, N, and PI are not available, nor
   are the other usages of the names X and NO. *)
   END.
```

Errors can occur as a result of unintentional use of global variables. Suppose, for instance, that you are in the habit of using the variable I as the index of FOR loops. If you use a FOR loop in both the main program and in some procedure, but you forget to declare I in that procedure, there is no syntax error. The procedure will happily use the I declared for the main program (and probably mess up the main program). This is a common error; it is so common, in fact, that some Pascal compilers disallow the use of a global variable as the index of a FOR loop.

7.4 RETURNING VALUES FROM FUNCTIONS

A value is returned from a function by assigning that value to the name of the function.

```
FUNCTION SUM(A, B: INTEGER): INTEGER;
    BEGIN
    SUM: = A + B
    END;
```

In the course of computing the function, you may assign an initial value to the function name, then change it one or more times. The value actually returned by the function is the value the function name has when the function is finished.

```
TYPE
        ARY: ARRAY [1..10] OF INTEGER;

FUNCTION INARRAY(KEY: INTEGER; A: ARY): BOOLEAN;
    VAR
            I: INTEGER;
    BEGIN
            INARRAY: = FALSE;
            FOR I: = 1 TO 10 DO
                IF A[I] = KEY THEN INARRAY: = TRUE
    END;
```

Pascal allows recursive functions. That is, it is legal for a function to call itself. The example commonly given is that of a factorial: the factorial of a positive integer N is the product of all the integers 1..N.

```
1    FUNCTION FACTORIAL(N: INTEGER): INTEGER;
2        BEGIN
3            IF N = 1 THEN FACTORIAL: = 1
4            ELSE FACTORIAL: = N * FACTORIAL (N – 1)
5        END;
```

Proper use of recursion will be discussed in Section 7.6. Our concern here is that the name FACTORIAL is used in two different ways in line 4. The first use, to the left of the : = , is to assign the function a value. The second use, as FACTORIAL(N – 1), is a recursive call. Pascal must be able to distinguish these two uses.

Rule: The function is given a value by using the function name as the left-hand side of an assignment statement; in any other position the function name acts as a recursive call.

```
TYPE
        ARY: ARRAY[1..10] OF INTEGER;
```

```
FUNCTION ARYSUM (A: ARY): INTEGER;
    VAR
        I: INTEGER;
    BEGIN
        ARYSUM:=0;
        FOR I:=1 TO 10 DO
            ARYSUM:=ARYSUM+A[I]                    (* Error *)
    END;
```

The line marked as an error contains an unintentional recursive call to ARYSUM. The computer will print an error message because ARYSUM is being called with the wrong number (zero) of parameters, but it will not detect the true error.

The general solution is to use an extra local variable to hold the value of the function during computation, and to assign this value to the function name as the last action of the function.

```
FUNCTION ARYSUM(A: ARY): INTEGER;
    VAR
        I, RESULT: INTEGER;
    BEGIN
        RESULT:=0;
        FOR I:=1 TO 10 DO
            RESULT:=RESULT+A[I];
        ARYSUM:=RESULT
    END;
```

A function may return only a simple type (INTEGER, REAL, BOOLEAN, CHAR, subrange, or enumeration type), or a pointer. It may not return an ARRAY, STRING, RECORD, SET, or FILE.

7.5 FORWARD AND EXTERN DIRECTIVES

Pascal requires all identifiers to be declared before they are used. In particular, definitions of routines must precede use of those routines. The following is therefore illegal.

```
PROCEDURE A;
    BEGIN
        B          (* Illegal—B isn't defined yet. *)
    END;
PROCEDURE B;
    . . .
```

In this example the problem may be solved simply by putting Procedure B before Procedure A.

The simple solution does not work in the case of mutually recursive routines: where there is a group of routines, each of them calling some of the others. (If you are not a heavy user of recursion, mutual recursion may sound absurd to you. Yet for some problems, such as writing a compiler, mutual recursion is extremely useful.)

Reordering your routines may also be unsatisfactory when you have a strong preference for some particular order, say, logical or alphabetical. Pascal provides a partial solution to this problem by allowing you to declare a routine with a special keyword, called a directive, in place of the routine body; the actual routine body is postponed to some later point in the program.

Before the routine is used, declare it with the usual header line, but in place of the declarations and routine body, put the directive FORWARD. Later in the program you can put the declarations and body, preceded by an abbreviated header which omits the parameter list and (in the case of a function) omits the type of its returned value. For convenience in working on the program, the omitted information should be put into a comment.

```
FUNCTION PRIME(N: INTEGER): BOOLEAN;
    FORWARD;
. . .
(* Function PRIME may be used here. *)
. . .
FUNCTION PRIME;        (* (N: INTEGER): BOOLEAN *)
    VAR
        I, ROOT: INTEGER;
    BEGIN
        I: = 2;
        ROOT: = TRUNC(SQRT(N));
        WHILE (N MOD I <> 0) AND (I < ROOT) DO
            I: = I + 1;
        IF N = 2 THEN PRIME: = TRUE
                ELSE PRIME: = (N MOD I <> 0)
    END;
```

A similar construction is often used to link to external (separately compiled) subprograms. Linkage to external routines is not defined in Standard Pascal, but any implementation intended for serious use will provide such linkage.

In order to use an external routine, you must supply the header line as usual. (Pascal needs this information.) The body is replaced by a directive indicating that the routine is external. Since different languages have different linkage conventions, the directive used is often the name of the language that the external routine is written in.

```
FUNCTION RANDOM(X: REAL): REAL;
    FORTRAN;
```

Since linkage to external routines is not defined in Standard Pascal, every implementation does it differently. In Pascal 8000, the directives you may use are FORTRAN, PASCAL, and EXTERN (EXTERN means the same as PASCAL). In CDC Pascal, the directives are FORTRAN and EXTERN (here EXTERN means the same as FORTRAN). In PASLC you use EXTERN PASCAL, EXTERN ALGOL, EXTERN COBOL, or EXTERN FORTRAN. In UCSD Pascal, the directive EXTERNAL refers to an assembly language routine or to a separately compiled Pascal routine.

7.6   RECURSION

In Pascal a routine may call itself. Such a routine is said to be "recursive." In this section we provide a brief glimpse of the use of recursion, and give some guidelines for its use.

Recursion is useful primarily when a problem can be broken down into subproblems which have the same form as the original problem. We use recursion to solve the simpler problems, then put the results together to obtain a solution of the original problem.

Consider the problem of searching an ordered array for a particular value (the "key"). For simplicity, we will assume that the key does occur in the array. Since the array is in order, we can perform a "binary search" on the array, as follows. Compare the key to the middle element of the array; if they are equal, we are done. If the key is smaller than the middle element, search the left half of the array; if larger, search the right half.

Our first cut at the code looks like this.

```
CONST
      TABLESIZE = 100;
TYPE
      TABLE = ARRAY [1..TABLESIZE] OF INTEGER;
VAR
      A:    TABLE;

FUNCTION FIND(KEY: INTEGER; T: TABLE): INTEGER;
      (* KEY must occur in ordered array T. Find it and return its location. *)
      VAR
            MID: INTEGER;
      BEGIN
            MID: = TABLESIZE DIV 2;
            IF KEY = T[MID] THEN
                  FIND: = MID
            ELSE IF KEY < T[MID] THEN
                  (* search T[1] through T[MID – 1] for KEY *)
            ELSE (* KEY > T[mid] *)
```

(∗ search T[MID + 1] through T[TABLESIZE] for KEY ∗)
END;

Clearly, searching either the left- or the right-half of the array can be done by a binary search, and we already have most of a routine (FIND) to do that. However, FIND is currently designed to search within the bounds 1..TABLESIZE, and we will need to be able to search within arbitrary bounds. We can fix this by supplying the bounds explicitly as parameters, and using

FIND(KEY,A,1,TABLESIZE)

as our top-level call. Finishing the routine, we get

```
FUNCTION FIND(KEY: INTEGER; T: TABLE;
              LOW, HIGH: INTEGER): INTEGER;
     (∗ KEY must occur in the ordered array T in some location between
        T[LOW] and T[HIGH], inclusive. Find KEY and return its location. ∗)
VAR
     MID: INTEGER;
BEGIN
     MID: = (LOW + HIGH) DIV 2;
     IF KEY = T[MID] THEN
          FIND: = MID
     ELSE IF KEY < T[MID] THEN
          FIND: = FIND(KEY, T, LOW, MID − 1)
     ELSE (∗ KEY > T[MID] ∗)
          FIND: = FIND(KEY, T, MID + 1, HIGH)
END;
```

A Reminder: In the assignment statement FIND: = FIND(...), the right-hand side is a recursive call to FIND; the use of FIND on the left-hand side is to assign this invocation of the function a value to be returned. Remember also that LOW and HIGH are passed by value, so whatever the recursive call does with them, it cannot hurt the calling routine.

To really understand this function requires a leap of faith. That leap is this: as you read the function FIND, you must assume that the calls it makes to FIND work and return the correct values. If the function is correct at this level, it must also be correct at the lower levels of the recursion.

Too often people have tried to understand recursion by "looking down" into the recursion, and trying to unwind the various levels. The human mind is not built to cope with this. Rather, you must treat the recursive call as you would a call to any other routine. Assume (tentatively) that the called routine does its job properly, and use the results it ought to give to continue checking this routine. Once you can do this, recursion becomes simple and natural. If it helps, think of the recursive calls to FIND as being calls to "some other FIND routine" which does the same thing as ours, but which is known to work.

Once you have mastered the above conceptual leap, reading and debugging a recursive routine is just like reading and debugging any other routine. All the same errors can occur. In addition, there are three, and only three, new types of error that can occur.

First, you must make sure that whenever a routine recurs, it is with a simpler subproblem. If the routine recurs with an equally hard (or harder) problem, the recursion could go on forever. In the above example, whenever we made a recursive call to FIND, it was with a shorter segment of the array. For this problem, simpler means shorter.

Second, the routine must solve the very simplest problems itself, without resorting to recursion. Problems cannot be simplified indefinitely. Sooner or later, real work must be done.

In FIND the work was done by looking at one element of the array (the middle element). Since we assumed KEY did appear in the array, if the array segment is of size one (LOW = HIGH), T[MID] has to be equal to KEY, and no recursive call is made.

If perchance KEY does not appear in T, the above program may recur indefinitely. When this happens, LOW becomes larger than HIGH (convince yourself of this), so we can use this fact to stop the recursion and return a special value (say, 0) to indicate that KEY is not in T.

```
IF   LOW > HIGH THEN
        FIND:=0
ELSE
        BEGIN
        (* code developed previously *)
        END
```

The third thing that can go wrong is if the routine changes the values of any global variables or VAR parameters. It is not an error to do so; but whereas each level of a recursion has its own copies of any value parameters and local variables, there is only one copy of any global variable or VAR parameter, and this one instance is shared by all levels of the recursion. Hence, if a global variable or VAR parameter is altered, it is altered for everybody, at all levels of the recursion, and you have little choice but to try to work through the multiple levels of recursion to see if its value is correct at every point. This quickly causes the routine to become incomprehensible.

For example, each level of FIND has its own variable MID to work with, and each MID is independent of all the others. Hence you can work through FIND without worrying about what effect those recursive calls have on MID. The same holds true for each of the parameters and is especially important for LOW and HIGH, which have different values at different levels of recursion. In contrast, the array T is never altered, and could be a global or a VAR parameter with no loss of clarity (and perhaps considerable gain in efficiency).

Recursion is a powerful tool for solving certain types of problems, and should be in the repertoire of every professional programmer. In a way, we have barely scratched the surface of the topic; but if you learn to understand and to use recursion in the manner described here, everything else follows naturally.

7.7   PROCEDURES AND FUNCTIONS AS PARAMETERS

We have discussed only two types of parameters: call-by-value parameters (default), and call-by-reference parameters (indicated by the keyword VAR). There are two additional types: procedural parameters and functional parameters. These are defined in Standard Pascal but are not implemented often; neither PASLC nor UCSD Pascal permits them.

Note that passing a function as a parameter is different from functional composition. The following is an example of functional composition.

```
X := SQRT(SIN(Y))
```

Here, the SIN function is not passed to SQRT as a parameter. Rather, the value of SIN(Y) is computed, and that value is passed to SQRT. SQRT never knows it was given anything other than a number.

Contrasted with this, suppose we wanted to write a procedure PLOT which, given a function, would produce a plot of that function's values between LOW and HIGH. We might use the call

```
PLOT(SIN, LOW, HIGH)
```

Here, no value of SIN is computed. SIN itself is passed to PLOT as a parameter. Presumably, PLOT will proceed to call SIN a number of times.

There are two ways to declare procedural and functional parameters: the old way and the new way. We give the old way first.

In the formal parameter list, declare a procedural parameter by

```
PROCEDURE name
```

where the *name* is the alias that you will use for the procedure inside the routine. Functional parameters are similar, except that you must also specify the type of value returned by the function.

```
FUNCTION name : type
```

To continue with the PLOT example, suppose that we want to plot the graph sideways, with zero values falling at (about) column 20, and each column representing a step of 0.1 units. We further want to plot values of the function at intervals of 0.1 (for example, at LOW, LOW + 0.1, LOW + 0.2, etc.)

```
PROCEDURE PLOT(FUNCTION F: REAL; LOW, HIGH: REAL);
    VAR
        X, Y: REAL;
        SPACES: INTEGER;
    BEGIN
        X: = LOW;
        WHILE X < = HIGH DO
            BEGIN
            Y: = F(X);
            SPACES: = ROUND(10*Y + 20);
            WRITELN(' ':SPACES, '*');
            X: = X + 0.1
            END
    END;
```

F is used inside PLOT as if it were the real function name, but if PLOT is called as above, each call of F is actually a call to the SIN function.

The above procedure should work in Standard Pascal, but in both CDC Pascal and Pascal 8000 the built-in functions such as SIN are illegal as parameters. To get around this, you would do

```
FUNCTION MYSIN(X: REAL): REAL;
    BEGIN
        MYSIN: = SIN(X)
    END;
    . . .
PLOT(MYSIN, LOW, HIGH)
```

One final point: Procedures and functions used as parameters must not have VAR parameters. The above example works fine with SIN (or MYSIN), but it would not work with a function declared as, for example,

```
FUNCTION SINFUL(VAR X: REAL): REAL
```

The old method of passing functional and procedural parameters described above has a flaw: Pascal is unable to check that the parameters used for the functional or procedural parameter are legal. In the above example, PLOT contained the statement

```
Y := F(X)
```

which is fine because SIN expects one real parameter; but if PLOT had instead made the call

```
Y := F('PIGS IN A TREE', 3)
```

Pascal could not have told you that you had the wrong number of parameters, or that they were of the wrong type.

To fix this problem, the new Draft ANSI Standard for Pascal requires that declarations of functional and procedural parameters contain parameter lists showing the number and types of parameters they use, as follows.

PROCEDURE (*list_of_types*)
FUNCTION (*list_of_types*) : *type*

So in the new method you would change the function header of PLOT from

PROCEDURE PLOT(FUNCTION F: REAL; *other parameters*)

to

PROCEDURE PLOT(FUNCTION F(REAL): REAL; *other parameters*)

and now PLOT can check the parameters on calls to F.

This is a new change to Pascal. If your compiler allows functional and procedural parameters at all, chances are it still uses the old method.

Chapter 8

INPUT/OUTPUT

Pascal supports both high-level and low-level input/output. High-level I/O is easy to use, provided you are not too fussy about data formats. Low-level I/O is more work, but gives you more flexibility. Standard Pascal does not support interactive I/O. Thus every implementation which provides interactive I/O does it differently.

8.1 SIMPLE INPUT/OUTPUT

The intent of this section is to present in one place just enough information to allow you to begin using Pascal I/O. For more comprehensive information, refer to the later sections of this chapter.

First, if you are using a Pascal which has a PROGRAM header (for example, Pascal 8000 or UCSD Pascal), then begin your program with the line

PROGRAM *name* (INPUT,OUTPUT);

where *name* is any legal identifier (which should be chosen to help you remember what the program does). If your Pascal does not have program headers, then skip this line.

INPUT and OUTPUT are Standard Pascal names which are associated with the standard system files. (On the IBM 360/370, for example, these will be SYSIN and SYSPRINT.) No further effort on your part is required—in particular, INPUT and OUTPUT should not be declared in the VAR section.

Data are input by calling the standard procedure READ as follows.

READ (*list_of_variables*)

This is a free-format read. That is, you cannot specify which columns of which line are to be read; blanks and newlines are skipped over and ignored. This makes input very simple.

For example, if X, Y, and Z are of type REAL and N is integer, you might write

```
READ(X, Y, Z, N)
```

and provide the data

```
1.0
 2.0
3.0     12
```

and this will assign X: = 1.0, Y: = 2.0, Z: = 3.0, N: = 12. Note that input values are separated by blanks and newlines, not by commas.

You may read only constants of types REAL, INTEGER, and CHAR. Arrays and records containing these types may be read on an element-by-element basis.

```
VAR
    A: ARRAY[1..ARRAYSIZE] OF INTEGER;
    R: RECORD
            X, Y: REAL
        END;
    ...
    FOR I: = 1 TO ARRAYSIZE DO READ(A[I]);
    READ(R.X, R.Y)
```

To output information, use the standard procedure WRITELN.

WRITELN (*list_of_expressions*)

The expressions in the *list_of_expressions* may be simple or complex, but each must result in a value of type INTEGER, REAL, CHAR, BOOLEAN, or PACKED ARRAY OF CHAR. UCSD Pascal also allows output of LONG INTEGERs and STRINGs, but does not support output of BOOLEAN values. The values are written on a single line, followed by a newline. (On many systems, newline is a carriage return and a linefeed.) For example,

WRITELN(' THE SUM OF ', X, ' AND ', Y, ' IS ', X + Y)

WRITELN may be used without parameters (or parentheses) to write a blank line.

UCSD Pascal writes out numbers without leading or trailing blanks, so to prevent consecutive numbers from running together you must take care to put quoted blanks between them in the output list. Other versions of Pascal will write out all but the very longest numbers with leading blanks.

Many line printers use the first character of a line as a carriage control character. If your output file is being sent to a line printer, you should make sure that each line begins with a blank. Other carriage control characters are discussed in Section 8.3.

The following program illustrates simple input and output. It assumes that numbers are output with leading blanks, so that no explicit carriage control is necessary.

```
PROGRAM SQUAREROOTS (INPUT, OUTPUT);
VAR
        I, N: INTEGER;
BEGIN
        REPEAT
                READ(N);
                FOR I:=1 TO N DO
                        WRITELN(I, SQRT(I));
                WRITELN
        UNTIL N = 0
END.
```

8.2   FILES

Files are collections of data external to the program. If your program reads cards, those cards are considered to form a file. If your program produces printed output, the information printed forms a file. If your program reads directly from a keyboard, the keyboard itself is considered to be a file.

There are two kinds of files. External files are those which have an existence independent of your program. Local files are created and used by the program, but disappear again before the program finishes. External files are used for "real" I/O, that is, reading previously existing data into the program, and writing results that will not vanish when the program terminates. Local files may involve real I/O, such as to a disk file, but they are used for temporary storage by the program, just as you might use an array.

Pascal provides two standard external files, INPUT and OUTPUT. In a batch-oriented system, INPUT will generally refer to the data deck (on cards) which follows your program, and OUTPUT will refer to the results sent to the line printer. In UCSD Pascal, which is fully interactive, INPUT refers to the keyboard and OUTPUT refers to the CRT screen.

On the IBM 360/370, the standard system names for the input and output files are SYSIN and SYSPRINT, respectively. You still use the Pascal names INPUT and OUTPUT within your program, and the operating system will see to it that INPUT=SYSIN and OUTPUT=SYSPRINT. On both the DEC-10 and the CDC, the system names are the same as the Pascal names, so that the Pascal names INPUT and OUTPUT refer to actual files named INPUT and OUTPUT, respectively.

Both the CDC and the DEC-10 compilers have an additional standard external file TTY that is used for interactive I/O. When used for input, TTY refers to the keyboard; when used for output, TTY refers to the CRT screen.

In UCSD Pascal there is an additional standard file KEYBOARD which, like INPUT, is used for reading from the keyboard. The difference is that when you read from INPUT, any characters which are typed are automatically displayed on the screen, but when you read from KEYBOARD they are not.

Files are defined in two places in your program: in the PROGRAM header, and in the VAR section. The general rules for declaring files are.

1 Declare the standard files (INPUT, OUTPUT, and perhaps others) you play to use in the PROGRAM header, if you have one. Do not declare standard files in a VAR part. (NOTE: Many implementations require you to declare OUTPUT, even if you do not plan to use it, so that the system has some place to put error messages.)

2 Declare any nonstandard external files in both the PROGRAM header (if you have one) and in a VAR part.

3 Declare any local files in the appropriate VAR part, but not in the PROGRAM header.

Of the systems considered in this book, Pascal 8000 follows this scheme exactly, CDC Pascal and PASLC do not have PROGRAM headers, and UCSD Pascal has a program header but ignores any file names you put in it.

The form of a PROGRAM header is

PROGRAM *program_name* (*list_of_files*)

where *program_name* is a name of your choice, and is not used for any purpose other than to remind you what the program does. The *list_of_files* contains zero or more file names, separated by commas. (If your system lets you get away with no file names at all, leave out the parentheses too.)

Example:

PROGRAM ORBIT (INPUT, UPDATES, OUTPUT, REALDATA)

The form of a file declaration in the VAR part is

list_of_files : FILE OF *type*

where the *list_of_files* consists of one or more names, separated by commas, and the *type* refers to the type of data read from or written to the file. Often the type is CHAR, so that the file is readable to humans; but you could have, for example, a FILE OF REAL, so that the information on the file consists

entirely of real numbers in binary format. The standard files INPUT, OUT-
PUT, and (if available) TTY are predefined to be of type FILE OF CHAR.

The type name TEXT is often used as a synonym for FILE OF CHAR.

Examples:

```
VAR
     UPDATES: TEXT;
     REALDATA: FILE OF REAL;
```

A file can be either an input file or an output file. An input file is one
form which the program can receive data, such as INPUT. An output file is
one to which the program can send data. In Standard Pascal, no file may be
simultaneously an input and an output file, but it can be an input file at one
time and an output file at another. (There are exceptions to this rule on
specific systems, such as TTY on the DEC-10, which acts as both an input
and an output file.)

Once your files are declared, you can begin using them. The system
automatically opens and closes the standard files for you (and it is usually
illegal for you to attempt to open them yourself), but for nonstandard files
there is a three-step sequence you should follow.

1 Open the file for reading or for writing.
2 Read from the file or write to it. This may involve multiple calls to
  READ and READLN, or to WRITE and WRITELN, scattered
  throughout your program.
3 Close the file when you are done using it.

To open a file for reading, use the procedure call RESET(*filename*).
This resets the file to the beginning. If the file is already open, this call will
close it (terminating any pending I/O), reset it to the beginning, and open it
again.

To open a file for writing, use the procedure call REWRITE(*filename*).
This discards any previous contents of the file, making it empty, and opens
the file for writing.

RESET and REWRITE work slightly differently in UCSD Pascal, because file names used by the UCSD system may contain periods and other
special characters. Both RESET and REWRITE take a second parameter,
which is a string whose value is the name to be used as the name of the file
by the UCSD system. For example,

```
SOURCE: = 'DATA.TEXT';
RESET(MYFILE, SOURCE);
REWRITE(DUMPFILE, 'PRINTER:');
```

In each case the first parameter is the name used by the program for the file, while the second parameter is the name used by the UCSD system for that same file.

In UCSD Pascal you may RESET a file that is already open, using RESET with only the first parameter. It is illegal to use REWRITE or to use RESET with two parameters on a file that is already open. However, you may close the file (see below), and then open it again.

While the file is open, you may use it for input or output, as appropriate. The remaining sections of this chapter give further details on how to read and write files.

Pascal automatically closes all files for you when the program terminates. UCSD allows you to close a file yourself and, in fact, it is usually necessary to close and "lock" any diskette files you have written. To do this, use one of the procedure calls

> CLOSE (*filename*)

or

> CLOSE (*filename, option*)

where *option* is one of NORMAL, LOCK, PURGE, or CRUNCH.

NORMAL just closes the file. This is the way that Pascal would do it for you automatically when the program terminates. Unfortunately, if the file is a diskette file that you opened with REWRITE and then wrote to, the file disappears.

LOCK makes the file permanent. This is the option you should use if the file is a diskette file that you want to have after the program is finished.

PURGE makes the file disappear. If you already had a diskette file with the same name, it is unchanged. If the file is a device name, the device will go off-line.

CRUNCH is used to modify an input file. If the file has been only partially read, and is closed with CRUNCH, any information not yet read from the file into the buffer variable (see Section 8.6) will be deleted from the file. CRUNCHing a textfile will leave it in an inconsistent state. For a file being written, CRUNCH does the same thing as LOCK.

8.3   HIGH-LEVEL INPUT/OUTPUT FOR TEXTFILES

High-level I/O is provided by the four standard procedures READ, READLN, WRITE, and WRITELN. (Note that these are procedure calls, not statements.)

To input information from a textfile that is, a FILE OF CHAR, use one of the two following procedures.

READ (*textfile* , *list_of_variables*)

or

READLN (*textfile* , *list_of_variables*)

If the *textfile* is the standard file INPUT, it may be omitted. The variables in the *list_of_variables* are separated by commas. They are not restricted to simple variables, but may be components of (nonpacked) arrays or records. Thus, given the declaration

```
VAR
    A: ARRAY[1..10] OF REAL;
    R: RECORD
        X: ARRAY[1..10] OF INTEGER;
        Y: REAL
    END;
    MYDATA: TEXT        (* that is, FILE OF CHAR *)
```

one may write

```
FOR I := 1 TO 10 DO READ (A[I]);
READ (MYDATA, R.X[5], R.Y)
```

In Standard Pascal, only variables of type INTEGER, REAL, and CHAR may be read. For these, the operation of the READ procedure is as follows.

1 If the variable to be read is of type CHAR, then the next input character (whatever it may be) is read in and assigned to that variable.

2 If the variable is of type INTEGER or REAL, READ skips over and ignores any blanks and newlines (end-of-line markers), until it finds a character that is not a blank or newline. Then it reads and attempts to assemble into a numeric quantity whatever characters it finds. (An error may result if the input does not represent a valid number of the correct type.) The first character following the number has been "peeked at" (so Pascal can tell it has reached the end of the number), but it is left to be read by the next variable in the read list (or if none, then by the next READ.)

READLN operates exactly as READ, but adds the following step

3 After reading into the last variable in the read list, skip over and ignore any remaining characters until a newline has been read. Thus, the next read operation will commence at the beginning of the next line.

READLN may be used without any parameters (variables) to skip lines.

If the *textfile* name is also omitted, then omit the parentheses which normally enclose the list of variables.

    READLN

or

    READLN (*textfile*)

It is usually possible to call READ in the same way (without any list of variables), but this does not do anything.

Pascal 8000 adds to the above the ability to read the type PACKED ARRAY (. 1..*n* .) OF CHAR, and UCSD Pascal can read STRINGs. To read variables of any other type, you must write your own input procedure which reads characters, figures out which value they represent, and returns that value. Hints on doing this are given in the sections discussing the various data types.

To output information to a textfile, use the procedures

    WRITE (*textfile* , *list_of_expressions*)

or

    WRITELN (*textfile* , *list_of_expressions*)

If the *textfile* is OUTPUT, it may be omitted. The expressions in the *list_of_expressions* are separated by commas. Any expression, however complex, may be used, as long as its result is one of the types REAL, INTEGER, CHAR, BOOLEAN, or PACKED ARRAY [1..*n*] OF CHAR. In UCSD Pascal STRING values can also be written out.

Both WRITE and WRITELN compute the value of each expression, convert it into a sequence of characters (if numeric or Boolean), and output the characters to the specified file. WRITE does not write a newline following the last value, so that a subsequent call to WRITE or WRITELN will extend the line just written; WRITELN does write a newline following the last value.

It is a good idea, when using WRITE, to do a final WRITELN just before the program terminates. Some operating systems will lose the last line of output if it does not end in a newline.

WRITE and WRITELN provide the programmer with a modicum of control over the format of the output. An expression in the output list may be written as

    expression : *field_width*

where the *expression* yields the value to be printed, while the *field_width* is a positive integer expression that specifies how many character positions to use for the value. For example,

    WRITE (COUNT:5)

writes the value of COUNT with enough blanks preceding it to use exactly five characters on the output line.

Any *expression* in a call to WRITE or WRITELN may be followed by an integer *field_width*; the effect is to pad on the left with just enough blanks to yield the desired number of characters. If the value to be printed is numeric and is too large to fit in the *field_width* specified, Pascal usually will use as much space as is needed; this may make the output messy, but no information is lost. According to Standard Pascal, real numbers are always printed with at least one preceding blank, so this should be taken into account when specifying *field_width*.

Real numbers are normally written out in scientific notation, that is, with an exponent. To write reals out in standard notation, a second field is given following the *field_width*, to specify how many digits are to be printed to the right of the decimal point. The form is

real_expression : *field_width* : *fraction_length*

where *real_expression* yields the value to be printed, the *field_width* is the total number of character positions to be used, and the *fraction_length* tells how many of these positions to use for the fraction part. The *field_width* and the *fraction_length* are integer expressions. For example,

    PI: = 3.1415926536;
    WRITE (PI: 8: 4)

writes the following (where # indicates a blank).

    # #3.1416

If you do not specify field widths and fraction lengths the implementation supplies them. You can make reasonably neat tables of numbers without ever specifying field widths, because the implementation will not look at the value of the number when choosing a field width, but instead will use a fixed width which is large enough to print any value of a given type. In this way your columns will be widely spaced, but they will line up.

The default field width for type CHAR is 1, and the default width for a PACKED ARRAY [1..k] OF CHAR is k. Pascal 8000 uses a field width of 4 to print the Boolean value TRUE and field width 5 for FALSE. Most other Pascals will use the same field width (usually 6 or more) for either value.

Pascal provides the procedure PAGE(*textfile*), which will cause the next line written to the *textfile* to appear at the top of a new page (assuming that the output is printed on a suitable device). If the parameter is omitted, file OUTPUT is used.

Most line printers use the first character of each line for a carriage-control character. There is no standard for carriage control characters, but the following are in wide use.

blank   single space before printing

0 (zero)   double space before printing

1 (one)   skip to new page before printing

+   print without advancing paper (overprint)

When a line begins with an unrecognized carriage control, such as a letter, the line printer will usually single space. It may or may not print the letter.

It should be emphasized that carriage control is not a part of Pascal (or any other language), but is something done by the line printer. If you know what carriage controls to use for your line printer in some other language, you know them for Pascal.

8.4   INPUT/OUTPUT FOR OTHER TYPES OF FILES

The preceding section concerns only reading from and writing to a textfile, that is, a FILE OF CHAR. (Most implementations provide TEXT as a synonym for FILE OF CHAR.) Reading numbers from a textfile is not pure input: it also involves converting the numbers from an external representation (as a sequence of characters) to an internal representation (as a binary number). Similarly, writing numbers to a textfile involves converting them from binary to character representation.

You may also declare a file (in the VAR section) as

FILE OF *type*

where *type* is any type except a file, or a structured type containing a file as a component. In addition, it would not be wise to have a file of pointers or even a file of any type containing pointers. For example, suppose you had a type

```
NODE = RECORD
          VAL: INTEGER;
          NEXT: ↑ NODE
       END
```

and suppose you use this type to implement a linked list. If A and B are NODES, it might be that A.NEXT points to B. When you output A and B the value output for A.NEXT will be the machine address at which B currently resides. Unfortunately, when you input A and B again, they probably will not be in exactly the same machine locations as before, and A.NEXT will point to where B used to be, not where it is now. The pointer will be wrong. The problem of pointer input/output is a very difficult one, and has not been solved in any existing language.

Let us suppose that you have a file named FOO of type FILE OF TABLE, where a "TABLE" is some type you have defined in the TYPE section. You may WRITE to this file, and you may READ from the file, using procedure calls READ and WRITE as described earlier.

READ (*filename, list_of_variables*)
WRITE (*filename, list_of_ expressions*)

Now all the *variables* in the READ must be of type TABLE, and all the *expressions* in the WRITE must yield values of type TABLE, because that is what the file FOO has been defined to hold. (Of course, a TABLE may be a RECORD with fields of several different types.)

Such files can be very useful for holding large amounts of information, or for creating a file from one program that can be used by another. In particular, real numbers can be transmitted between programs without any loss in accuracy, because there will be no conversions to character code and back again.

Do not, however, list such a file to your terminal or to a line printer and expect the results to be readable. They will be in whatever binary representation your computer uses, and will look like garbage when listed.

READLN and WRITELN may be used only with textfiles. They differ from READ and WRITE only in the way they handle the newline character, and files of type other than CHAR cannot have a newline character (or any other character) as an element. In UCSD Pascal READ, READLN, WRITE, and WRITELN are ALL for use only with textfiles. You may have other types of files, as described above, but you use GET and PUT (see Section 8.6) to access them.

8.5   END-OF-DATA INDICATORS

When reading in a variable amount of data, it is necessary to know when to quit reading. There are three general ways of doing this.

1 Read under count control. The programmer must count the number of data items and tell the program how many there are.

```
POPULATION: = 0;
READ(N);
FOR I: = 1 TO N DO
     BEGIN
     READ(HEADCOUNT);
     POPULATION: = POPULATION + HEADCOUNT
     END;
```

The disadvantage of this method is that humans do not count as accurately as computers, and too many errors occur when N is much greater than ten.

A minor variation is to build the value of N directly into the program. This is poor style, as it makes the program less flexible.

2 Read until a sentinel is reached. A sentinel is a special data value which can be read in like an ordinary value, but which cannot legally appear in the actual data.

```
POPULATION:=0;
READ(HEADCOUNT);
WHILE HEADCOUNT <> −1 DO
    BEGIN
    POPULATION:=POPULATION+HEADCOUNT;
    READ(HEADCOUNT)
    END;
```

This method results in fewer errors than requiring the user to count data items, and is the preferred method when more than one group of data must be read. It does have the disadvantage that a suitable sentinel value must be found, and this is not always easy. Novice programmers who use this method sometimes make the mistake of using as sentinel a value that is not impossible, but merely unlikely.

3 Read until the end-of-file. The function EOF(*filename*) returns TRUE if an attempt has been made to read past the last item in the file; hence, it acts as an automatic sentinel. (If the *filename* is INPUT, it may be omitted.)

```
POPULATION:=0;
READ(HEADCOUNT);
WHILE NOT EOF DO
    BEGIN
    POPULATION:=POPULATION+HEADCOUNT;
    READ(HEADCOUNT)
    END;
```

This is the preferred method when only one group of data is to be read.

Another common problem is to read all the data on a single line of a textfile. In Pascal, a line consists of zero or more characters followed by a line terminator, called a "newline." The line terminator may consist of more than one character in the actual file (usually carriage return/line feed), but however it is represented, Pascal reads it in as if it were a single blank. This is convenient if you want to skip over blanks and newlines.

To distinguish a true blank from a blank that represents a newline,

Pascal provides the function EOLN(*textfile*). If the parameter *textfile* is omitted, INPUT is assumed. EOLN becomes true when the next character to be read is a newline. That is, EOLN answers the question, ''Is the character just read the last character before the newline?''

For example, given the declarations

```
VAR
    S: ARRAY [1..100] OF CHAR;
    N: INTEGER;
```

you can read a complete line as a sequence of characters, and count how many characters there are, with the code

```
N:=0;
WHILE NOT EOLN DO
    BEGIN
    N:=N+1;
    READ(S[N])
    END;
READLN;        (* to skip over the newline *)
```

Note that EOLN tests whether the last character on the line has been read. If you are doing numeric input, those numbers are represented as sequences of characters. If the number extends to the end of the line, EOLN works fine; but if there are trailing blanks, EOLN will tell you that you are not yet finished reading the line.

Using EOLN when doing numeric input is especially troublesome in two cases: (1) When your operating system insists on padding some or all lines with trailing blanks; (2) When you are doing interactive input (since a user might type an extra space before hitting the RETURN key).

8.6   LOW-LEVEL INPUT/OUTPUT

Pascal supplies two very simple primitives, GET and PUT, which do pure input/output, that is, input/output without any automatic conversions from strings to numeric, or *vice versa*. GET and PUT may be used along with or instead of the procedures READ and WRITE.

Consider the declaration of a file FOO,

```
VAR
    FOO: FILE OF T
```

where T may be any type except another file type. File FOO consists of a sequence of zero or more elements, all of type T. The number of elements in the file is called the ''length'' of the file; a file of length zero is said to be empty.

A file may be in either "read mode," so that it can be read from, or "write mode," so that it can be written to. A file cannot be in both modes at the same time.

Declaration of the file FOO has the side effect of introducing a new variable FOO↑ of type T. FOO↑ is called a "buffer variable", and usually has as its value one of the elements of file FOO (though it may have some other value, or its value may be undefined).

The notation FOO↑ resembles the notation used for pointer types, and it is sometimes convenient to think of FOO↑ as "pointing to" some element of file FOO, but this analogy can be misleading. FOO is a file, not a pointer, and FOO↑ is an oddly named variable of type T that is associated with FOO.

The following operations on FOO use or alter the value of FOO↑.

RESET(FOO)   Put FOO into read mode.
                If FOO is nonempty, FOO↑ is assigned the value of the first element of FOO, and EOF(FOO) becomes FALSE.
                If FOO is empty, FOO↑ becomes undefined and EOF(FOO) becomes TRUE.

GET(FOO)   If EOF(FOO) is FALSE, FOO↑ is assigned the value of the next element of FOO. If there is no next value, FOO↑ becomes undefined, and the value of EOF becomes TRUE.
                If EOF(FOO) is initially TRUE, then the effect of GET(FOO) is undefined.

REWRITE(FOO)   Put FOO in write mode. The current contents (if any) of FOO are discarded, and EOF(FOO) is set to TRUE.

PUT(FOO)   If EOF(FOO) is TRUE, the value of FOO↑ is appended to file FOO, FOO↑ becomes undefined, and EOF(FOO) remains TRUE.
                If EOF(FOO) is FALSE, the effect of PUT(FOO) is undefined.

If X is a variable of type T, then

READ(FOO, X)   is equivalent to   X:=FOO↑ ; GET(FOO)
WRITE(FOO, X)   is equivalent to   FOO↑ := X; PUT(FOO)

As an example of input, consider the problem of reading a single line containing from 0 to 20 integers. The line may or may not have leading and trailing blanks. We use READ to do input with numeric conversion, and

GET to skip blanks up to but not including the next nonblank character.

```
VAR
    A: ARRAY [1..20] OF INTEGER;
    N: INTEGER;
. . .
N:=0;
WHILE NOT EOLN DO
    IF INPUT↑ = ' ' THEN GET(INPUT)
    ELSE
        BEGIN
        N:=N+1;
        READ(A[N])
        END;
READLN;        (* skip over the newline *)
```

8.7 INTERACTIVE INPUT/OUTPUT

In UCSD Pascal the files INPUT, OUTPUT, and KEYBOARD are of file type INTERACTIVE, and nothing special needs to be done. (KEYBOARD is the same as INPUT, except that the characters typed by the user do not appear on the television monitor.) In Pascal 8000, interactive I/O does not exist.

Both CDC Pascal and PASLC on the DEC-10 use a standard file TTY for interactive I/O. TTY is a predefined file, and should not be declared again in the VAR section. (Neither Pascal uses a program header, so TTY need not be declared there.)

Normally, output goes into a holding area called a "buffer," and accumulates there until there is enough to be worth printing. This is a problem for interactive I/O, because your output does not appear when you intend it to. The effect you see is that the computer keeps asking for input but does not seem to be producing any output.

To solve this problem, DEC-10 Pascal and CDC Pascal both provide a procedure BREAK, which forces the contents of the TTY output buffer to be sent to your terminal. Normal use of BREAK is to put it after any output to TTY that demands a response. For instance,

```
(* PROGRAM BREAKEXAMPLE(TTY); *)
VAR
    X, Y: INTEGER;
BEGIN
    WRITELN(TTY, 'HELLO. I CAN ADD INTEGERS.');
    REPEAT
```

```
            WRITE(TTY, 'GIVE ME AN INTEGER: ');
            BREAK;
            READ(TTY, X);
            WRITE(TTY, 'NOW GIVE ME ANOTHER: ');
            BREAK;
            READ(TTY, Y);
            WRITELN(TTY, 'THE SUM IS ', X + Y);
            WRITELN(TTY)
        UNTIL FALSE
END.
```

The use of WRITE rather than WRITELN allows the answer to be typed in on the same line as the question.

Another minor quirk is that both RESET and READLN will, when used, attempt to read ahead one character and put it in the input buffer. For interactive use, this means that the system will try to read a character that the user has not yet been given a chance to type.

The solution in UCSD Pascal is to define a new file type, INTERACTIVE. For a file declared as an INTERACTIVE, the reading of the next character is deferred until the user requests input, so the problem seldom arises. (It may happen, though, if the program uses the buffer variables INPUT↑ or KEYBOARD↑.) This way of doing the input is called "lazy I/O," because the work of doing the input is put off as long as possible.

For PASLC and CDC Pascal, the solution is in two parts. First, Pascal will automatically do a RESET(TTY) at the beginning of your program (if you declare TTY), so the first thing your program will do is halt and wait for input. Hit the RETURN key once to satisfy it, and write your program to expect that the first line it reads from TTY will begin with a blank. Second, never do a READLN from TTY; use READ instead. Alternatively, you can skip READ and READLN entirely, and do only low-level input from TTY, using procedure GET(TTY) and buffer variable TTY↑.

If you have not used interactive I/O before, there is one style rule you must learn: never do a READ without first letting the user know what information you are expecting of him. It can be very disconcerting to have the program stop and wait for input when you have no idea what it wants to know, and have no way to ask it.

Finally, notice the deliberate use of an infinite loop. This is quite common in interactive computing, as there is always some system-defined way of stopping a program when you tire of it. How useful infinite loops are depends on how gracious the system is about letting you stop the program.

If you are paying for computer time, be sure to execute at least one READ each time through an infinite loop, so that if you somehow lose contact with the computer, it will pause at the READ instead of doing an infinite amount of work.

8.8   SEGMENTED FILES (CDC PASCAL ONLY)

In CDC Pascal, files may be segmented, so that the file consists of a sequence of segments (or records, in CDC terminology). Such a file is declared as

SEGMENTED FILE OF *type*

For example, a SEGMENTED FILE OF REAL might have the structure

```
                          ⎧ real
           ⎧ segment      ⎨ real
           ⎪              ⎩ real
   file   ⎨  segment      { real
           ⎪  segment      ⎧ real
           ⎩               ⎨ real
```

A file of characters might have those characters grouped into lines, with an arbitrary number of lines per segment, so the structure is more complex.

```
                                    ⎧ char
                       ⎧ line       ⎨ char
                       ⎪            ⎩ eoln
           ⎧ segment  ⎨             ⎧ char
           ⎪           ⎪            ⎪ char
           ⎪           ⎩ line       ⎨ char
   file   ⎨                         ⎪ char
           ⎪                        ⎩ eoln
           ⎪                        ⎧ .        .
           ⎩ segment   { .          ⎨ .        .
                                    ⎩ .        .
```

To write out a segmented file, use WRITE, WRITELN, or PUT as usual, and call procedure PUTSEG(*file*) when you are done writing each segment.

The procedure REWRITE(*file*) discards the current contents of the file and opens it for writing, as usual. REWRITE(*file*, *n*) moves the file position to the beginning of the *n*th segment forward from the current position (*n* may be zero or negative for a backward move), discards the remainder of the file, and opens it for further writing.

To read a segmented file, begin by calling RESET(*file*) to open the file for reading. This positions the buffer pointer so that you are ready to read the first datum in the first segment of the file.

Once the file is opened, use READ, READLN, or GET as usual. After each of these input requests, call function EOS(*file*) to find out if the input request failed. EOS(*file*) becomes TRUE when the request for input failed because an end of segment was reached. If EOF(*file*) has also become TRUE, there is no next segment; otherwise, call GETSEG(*file*) to begin reading that next segment.

GETSEG may be called with a second parameter. GETSEG(*file*, *n*) positions the buffer to point at the beginning of the *n*th segment forward of the current position. GETSEG(*file*,1) is equivalent to GETSEG(*file*). GET-SEG(*file*,0) restarts reading of the current segment. A negative value for *n* causes a backward move.

The following code can be used to copy a segmented character file.

```
VAR
      SOURCE, DEST: SEGMENTED FILE OF CHAR;
      CH: CHAR;
. . .
RESET(SOURCE); RESET(DEST);
WHILE NOT EOF(SOURCE) DO
      BEGIN
      WHILE NOT EOS(SOURCE) DO
            BEGIN
            WHILE NOT EOLN(SOURCE) DO
                  BEGIN
                  READ(SOURCE, CH); WRITE(DEST, CH);
                  END;
            READLN(SOURCE); WRITELN(DEST);
            END;
      GETSEG(SOURCE); PUTSEG(DEST)
      END
```

PART THREE

STRUCTURED
DATA TYPES

Chapter 9

USER-DEFINED SCALAR TYPES

In Pascal terminology, a "scalar type" is one of the four simple (unstructured) types INTEGER, REAL, BOOLEAN, and CHAR. Pascal also provides a means for the user to define new scalar types.

9.1 DECLARING AND USING ENUMERATION TYPES

An enumeration type is described by enclosing a list of identifiers, separated by commas, in parentheses. This may be done wherever a type description is allowed, such as in the TYPE and VAR sections.

```
TYPE
      COLOR = (RED, YELLOW, GREEN, BLUE);
VAR
      PAINT, INK: COLOR;
      SEASON: (SUMMER, FALL, WINTER, SPRING);
```

Here two enumeration types have been declared. The first type is named COLOR; any variable of that type (such as INK) may have as its value one of the four constants RED, YELLOW, GREEN, and BLUE. The second enumeration type is an anonymous type (has no name), and SEASON is a variable of that type. SEASON may take on any of the values SUMMER, FALL, WINTER, and SPRING.

The names inside parentheses are constants of the corresponding enumeration type, and follow the usual rules for constants. For example, they may be used in expressions, and may not be altered. It is illegal to declare these names for any other purpose in the same block.

```
TYPE
      MOOD = (EXCITED, BORED, HAPPY, BLUE);          (* illegal *)
VAR
      RED: INTEGER;                                  (* illegal *)
```

BLUE cannot be both a COLOR constant and a MOOD constant, nor can RED be both a constant and a variable.

Enumeration variables may be assigned values.

```
PAINT:=BLUE;
INK:=PAINT;
```

Enumeration expressions and constants are allowed in CASE statements.

```
CASE SEASON OF
      SPRING:           CAVORT;
      SUMMER, FALL:     WORK;
      WINTER:           HIBERNATE
END;
```

The comparison operators $<$, $<=$, $>$, $>=$, $=$, $<>$ are defined for enumeration values of the same type. The ordering is that given in the type description, so that

```
RED < YELLOW < GREEN < BLUE
```

and

```
SUMMER < FALL < WINTER < SPRING.
```

It is illegal to attempt to compare enumeration constants or variables of different types.

```
IF WINTER < PAINT THEN . . .       (* illegal *)
```

Since enumeration values are ordered, it is possible to use subranges of an enumeration type.

```
TYPE
      COOLSEASON = FALL..SPRING;
VAR
      A: ARRAY [SUMMER..WINTER] OF INTEGER;
      B: ARRAY [COLOR] OF BOOLEAN;       (* RED..BLUE *)
```

Functions defined for use with enumeration types are

SUCC(x)   The next value after x. SUCC(x) is undefined if x is the last value.

PRED(x) The value just before x. PRED(x) is undefined if x is the first value.

ORD(x) The integer position of x in the list of enumeration constants, counting from zero.

For example, given that COLOR = (RED, YELLOW, GREEN, BLUE), we have

SUCC(RED) = YELLOW	PRED(RED) = undefined	ORD(RED) = 0
SUCC(YELLOW) = GREEN	PRED(YELLOW) = RED	ORD(YELLOW) = 1
SUCC(GREEN) = BLUE	PRED(GREEN) = YELLOW	ORD(GREEN) = 2
SUCC(BLUE) = undefined	PRED(BLUE) = GREEN	ORD(BLUE) = 3

SUCC and PRED are also defined for the scalar types INTEGER, BOOLEAN, and CHAR. ORD is also defined for BOOLEAN and CHAR.

Enumeration types provide excellent mnemonic aids. For example, if in your program you wish to classify different foreign countries according to their relationship to us, the enumeration constants (ENEMY, NEUTRAL, FRIENDLY) are far more meaningful than, say, the arbitrary values $-1, 0, 1$.

9.2   INPUT/OUTPUT FOR ENUMERATION VALUES

Pascal does not provide input/output of enumeration values. That is, given the declarations

```
TYPE
      COLOR = (RED, YELLOW, GREEN, BLUE);
VAR
      PAINT: COLOR;
```

there is no automatic way to read in the sequence of characters 'BLUE' and get the enumeration constant BLUE, nor can you say WRITE(PAINT) and get (say) the character string 'BLUE' written out. (You can, of course, declare a FILE OF COLOR, just as you can declare a file of almost any type, and you can do input/output of colors to that file. Such a file will not be in character format, however, so it will not be legible to humans; nor may it contain any other type of data).

If textfile I/O for enumeration values is sufficiently important to you, you can write your own I/O routines. The following routines for values of type COLOR can be used as models.

```
PROCEDURE WRITECOLOR (C: COLOR);
      BEGIN
            CASE C OF
                  RED:       WRITE (' RED ');
```

```
                    YELLOW:   WRITE (' YELLOW ');
                    GREEN:    WRITE (' GREEN ');
                    BLUE:     WRITE (' BLUE ');
            END
         END;

   PROCEDURE READCOLOR (VAR C: COLOR);
      VAR
          S:    PACKED ARRAY [1..6] OF CHAR;
          N:    INTEGER;
          CH:   CHAR;
      BEGIN
          REPEAT READ(CH) UNTIL CH <> ' ';   (* skip blanks *)
          N:=1;
          S[1]:=CH;
          REPEAT        (* pack characters into S *)
              N:=N+1;
              READ(CH);
              S[N]:=CH
          UNTIL (N = 6) OR (CH = ' ');
          FOR N := N+1 TO 6 DO S[N]:=' ';   (* pad with blanks *)
          IF S = 'RED   ' THEN C:=RED
          ELSE IF S = 'YELLOW' THEN C:=YELLOW
          ELSE IF S = 'GREEN ' THEN C:=GREEN
          ELSE IF S – 'BLUE   ' THEN C:=BLUE
          ELSE
              BEGIN
              WRITE (' *ERROR* INVALID INPUT COLOR: '");
              FOR I:=1 TO 6 DO WRITE (S[I]);
              WRITELN('"')
              END
      END;
```

Note: The variable CH is necessary because an element of a packed array may not be used as a VAR parameter, hence READ(S[N]) would be illegal.

9.3 SUBRANGE TYPES

New types may be formed by restricting the range of allowable values of INTEGER, CHAR, BOOLEAN, and enumeration types. Any such type is called a subrange type, and the type from which it is derived is called the parent type. The syntax is

least_value . . greatest_value

where the *least_value* is smaller than or equal to the *greatest_value*, according to the ordering defined on values of the parent type.

The ordering defined for integers is the obvious one. Characters are ordered according to the collating sequence (see Section 11.1 and Appendix C). Boolean values are ordered FALSE then TRUE, and enumeration values are ordered by their position in the enumerated list that defines them.

No specific operations are provided on subranges. Rather, they inherit all the operations available on the parent type. For example, you can multiply integers, therefore you can also multiply variables that are defined as subranges of the integers.

Subrange types can be used to conserve storage or to format storage in a particular way. They can also provide additional checks on the correctness of a program.

Subranges can conserve storage because fewer bits may be required for values in the restricted range. For example, on the IBM 370 an INTEGER value requires four bytes (32 bits) but a value limited to 0..255 requires only a single byte (8 bits). Pascal is not required to minimize the storage used for subrange variables, but most implementations will do so when the subrange variables occur as components of a packed structure.

The amount of storage required by a subrange variable is determined by the maximum and minimum values it could take on, rather than the range of those values. For example, a subrange declared as 200..203 requires eight bits, even though in theory two bits are sufficient to distinguish among four allowable values.

Subranges can be used in a packed record to specify the exact layout of that record at the bit level. For example, UCSD Pascal stores a date such as 25-DEC-82 in two bytes (16 bits) as follows.

```
TYPE
    DATE = PACKED RECORD
        MONTH: 1..12;          (* 4 bits *)
        DAY: 1..31;            (* 5 bits *)
        YEAR: 0..99            (* 7 bits *)
    END
```

Subranges can also provide added assurance that the program is correct, because the compiler can automatically insert checks to ensure that values stay within the specified limits. For example, if a DATE is defined as shown, a MONTH number of 14 would result in a runtime error message. Although error messages are not pleasant, they are usually better than failing to catch the error.

In many cases, however, use of a subrange variable will catch spurious errors that cause no harm but are a nuisance to fix. For example, the following code is supposed to determine whether array A contains a value KEY, and to set the Boolean variable FOUND to TRUE if the key is in the array and to FALSE otherwise. It works fine when range checking is turned off by a compiler option, but fails when range checking is done.

```
TYPE
    INDEX: 1..100;
VAR
    A: ARRAY[INDEX] OF INTEGER;
    KEY: INTEGER;
    FOUND: BOOLEAN;
    I: INDEX;
    ...
I := 1;
FOUND := FALSE;
REPEAT
    FOUND := (A[I] = KEY);
    I := I+1          (* range error occurs here *)
UNTIL FOUND OR (I > 100)
```

Note that an error will occur in the position marked, although no possible harm to the program can result. In particular, array location A[101] is never accessed. Moreover, the error is difficult to fix correctly. In deciding whether to use a subrange, we must balance the nuisance of repairing these spurious errors against the possible benefits of catching real errors.

It is not possible for Pascal to catch all errors involving subranges. For example,

```
VAR
    OCLOCK: 1..12;
PROCEDURE UPDOWN(VAR N: INTEGER);
    BEGIN
        N := N+1000;        (* error? *)
        N := N-1000
    END;
    ...
OCLOCK := 5;
UPDOWN(OCLOCK)
```

It is legal to call UPDOWN, which expects an integer parameter, with a subrange variable such as OCLOCK. This is because all operations on integers, including parameter transmission, are inherited by subranges of integers.

UPDOWN temporarily assigns OCLOCK the value 1005, which could overflow the storage allocated to OCLOCK. Even if it does not, the programmer must decide whether this constitutes a real error. UPDOWN cannot perform any error checking beyond that which it usually does for integers. The value of OCLOCK returned by UPDOWN may or may not be checked for legality by the calling routine, depending on your implementation.

Chapter 10

ARRAYS

Arrays in Pascal are much like arrays in other languages, though more flexibility is provided than in Basic or Fortran. Arrays may have any number of dimensions; the lower bounds are not always zero or always one, but are chosen by you; and you may have arrays containing any legal data type (except files). Pascal also checks that you do not go outside the declared bounds of your arrays. This is a minor nuisance at times, but protects you from a lot of very mysterious bugs.

10.1 ARRAY DECLARATIONS

The format of an array description is

ARRAY [*range_1, range_2, ..., range_N*] OF *type*

where each *range* specifies the set of possible values that the corresponding array subscript might take on, and *type* specifies the type of elements in the array.

For example,

ARRAY [1..10, −3..3] OF REAL

specifies a two-dimensional array of real numbers. The first subscript may take any value from 1 to 10, inclusive, while the second subscript may take any of the seven values from −3 to 3, inclusive. Thus the array holds ten times seven or 70 real numbers.

Pascal does not limit the number of dimensions an array may have. However, any computer has only a finite amount of memory, and multi-dimensioned arrays can use up space in a hurry. As in any language, you should figure out beforehand just how much space you are asking for, and keep your demands reasonable.

Recall that a type description may be used directly in the VAR section, or it may instead be given a name in the TYPE section, then the name of that type used in the VAR section. Thus the following are both legal.

```
VAR
     A: ARRAY [1..10, −3..3] OF REAL
```

and

```
TYPE
     ARY = ARRAY [1..10, −3..3] OF REAL;
VAR
     A: ARY
```

For reasons we will discuss shortly, the second form should be used for arrays which may be passed as parameters.

Subranges of integers may be given names in the TYPE section, so another way of writing the array declaration is

```
TYPE
     UPTOTEN = 1..10;
     ABS3 = −3..3;
VAR
     A: ARRAY [UPTOTEN, ABS3] OF REAL
```

or even

```
TYPE
     UPTOTEN: 1..10;
     ABS3: −3..3;
     ARY: ARRAY [UPTOTEN, ABS3] OF REAL;
VAR
     A: ARY
```

In addition to subranges of the integers, array subscripts may be BOOLEAN, subranges of Boolean (pretty useless), CHAR, subranges of CHAR, enumeration types, or subranges of enumeration types. The following example uses enumeration subscripts.

```
TYPE
     MAKE = (FORD, GM, CHRYSLER);
     STYLE = (SEDAN, WAGON, PICKUP, BUS);
VAR
     FLEET: ARRAY [MAKE, SEDAN..PICKUP] OF INTEGER
```

In this example MAKE stands for FORD..CHRYSLER, just as UPTOTEN stood for 1..10. The array FLEET thus has three ''makes'' by three ''styles'', hence nine entries.

An index range of BOOLEAN denotes FALSE..TRUE. An index range of CHAR includes all the characters in the collating sequence of the machine on which the program is run.

Different types of subscripts may be used for different dimensions in a single array, as in

```
VAR
    COUNT: ARRAY [MAKE, 1950..1990] OF INTEGER
```

All elements in an array must be of the same type. However, any previously defined type may be used, so you may have arrays of pointers, arrays of records, arrays of arrays, etc. For example,

```
TYPE
    PERSON = RECORD
        NAME: ARRAY [1..30] OF CHAR;
        AGE: 18..65;
        SALARY: REAL
    END;
VAR
    EMPLOYEE: ARRAY [1..50] OF PERSON
```

An array of arrays is defined to be equivalent to an array having additional dimensions. Thus you may write

```
VAR
    ARRAY [1..10] OF ARRAY [MAKE, STYLE] OF INTEGER
```

but this is really the same as

```
ARRAY [1..10, MAKE, STYLE] OF INTEGER
```

Arrays are normally stored with each element of the array beginning at a new word boundary (or a new byte boundary, on byte-oriented machines). This allows the array to be accessed quickly, but may waste storage space, particularly for arrays containing Booleans, enumeration types, or small subranges.

If storage space is critical, you may precede the keyword ARRAY by the keyword PACKED. This tells Pascal that you would like data values packed more than one to a word, if feasible, so that storage space is minimized at some cost in access time. The amount of storage space thus saved will vary from compiler to compiler; in fact, Pascal is free to ignore the word PACKED if it wishes.

In theory, whether an array is packed or not packed should not affect the correct operation of your program. In practice this is not always the case, because (1) a packed array is of a different type than an unpacked array, so this may affect assignment of entire arrays, and transmission of entire arrays as parameters, and (2) you cannot pass an element of a packed array as a VAR parameter to any routine, including the I/O routines.

10.2   ARRAY USAGE

Individual elements of an array may be referred to by using the name of the array, followed by a list of subscripts enclosed in square brackets. For example, given the declarations

```
VAR
    A, B: ARRAY [1..10] OF INTEGER;
    X: ARRAY [1..5, 1..100] OF INTEGER
```

the following statements are then legal:

```
A[5] := A[5] − 1;
B[N] := B[N]*X[3, 2];        (* assuming 1 <= N <= 10 *)
IF A[I] < A[J] THEN A[I] := A[I] + 1;
X[N, 3*N] := A[A[I]];
```

and so forth. Any expression, no matter how complex, may be used as an array subscript, as long as it evaluates to a value of the correct type within the correct range. Pascal does compile-time checking to ensure that array subscripts are of the correct type, and runtime checking to ensure that the values of the subscripts are in the specified range.

Pascal does not distinguish between multidimensioned arrays and singly dimensioned arrays of arrays (of arrays . . .). Thus the declaration of X given above is equivalent to the declaration

```
VAR
    X: ARRAY [1..5] OF ARRAY [1..100] OF INTEGER
```

so you could define X either way, and in either case it would be legal to refer to X[3, 50]. This same element could also be referred to as X[3][50], since the third element of X is an array of size 100; but the latter notation is awkward and never used.

The only operation defined for entire arrays is assignment. Given two arrays of exactly the same type, such as A and B above, one may be assigned to the other,

```
A := B
```

and this has the same meaning as

```
FOR I := 1 TO 10 DO
    A[I] := B[I]
```

To repeat: array assignment can only be performed when the two arrays are exactly the same type. This restriction is more severe that it might at first appear: the number of dimensions, the types and ranges of those dimensions, and the types of elements in the arrays must all be identical. In particular, if C is ARRAY [1..10] OF REAL and D is ARRAY [11..20] OF REAL, the assignment is still illegal. Sometimes the arrays may appear to be of identical types, yet the compiler will give an error message about type conflict. If this should happen, read Section 3.3 on type equivalence.

Note that no existing Pascal compiler is willing to consider a packed array to be of the same type as a nonpacked array. Hence presence or absence of the keyword PACKED in the array declaration can render array assignments illegal.

Arrays may be passed as parameters to routines (see Sections 3.3 and 7.2). The types of the arrays used as actual parameters must match those of the formal parameters.

10.3   USE OF FOR LOOPS

The FOR loop is the most important tool in manipulating arrays, as it provides an easy means of performing the same process on each and every element of the array. The examples which follow will assume the declarations

```
CONST
      M = 10;
      N = 10;
VAR
      A: ARRAY [1..N] OF INTEGER;
      B: ARRAY [1..M, 1..N] OF INTEGER;
```

The arrays may be zeroed out by the loops

```
FOR I : = 1 TO N DO A[I] : = 0
```

and

```
FOR I : = 1 TO M DO
      FOR J : = 1 TO N DO
            B[I, J] : = 0
```

Similarly, the largest element in A may be found by

```
MAX : = A[1];
FOR I : = 2 TO N DO
      IF A[I] > MAX THEN MAX : = A[I]
```

If we desire not the value of the largest element in A but rather its location, we may write:

```
MAXLOC := 1;
FOR I := 2 TO N DO
    IF A[I] > A[MAXLOC] THEN MAXLOC := I
```

These loops will work correctly even in the degenerate case of $N = 1$, since the FOR loops will not execute at all in this case.

Sometimes loops other than FOR loops are used with arrays. For example, it would not be appropriate to use a FOR loop to search an array A for a given value KEY, because we would normally want to exit the loop upon finding KEY, and not process the remaining elements of A. There is no safe way to get out of a FOR loop prematurely.

If KEY is known to be in array A, we could find (the first occurrence of) KEY as follows:

```
LOC := 1;
WHILE A[LOC] <> KEY DO LOC := LOC + 1
```

but this code will bomb if KEY is not in A because LOC will exceed N, the upper bound of A. A safer way to do the search is

```
FOUND := FALSE;         (* FOUND is Boolean *)
LOC  := 0;
WHILE (LOC < N) AND NOT FOUND DO
    BEGIN
    LOC := LOC + 1;
    FOUND := (A[LOC] = KEY)
    END
```

Upon exit, if FOUND is TRUE then LOC will be the location of A at which KEY was found.

Note that the comparison (A[LOC] = KEY) yields a value of TRUE or FALSE, and this value may be assigned directly to FOUND. This is more concise than the equivalent

```
IF A[LOC] = KEY THEN FOUND := TRUE ELSE FOUND := FALSE
```

and is actually more readable, once you get used to it. The parentheses are unnecessary but seem to improve readability.

Incidentally, beware of the following code, which is wrong for a rather subtle reason.

```
LOC := 1;
WHILE (I <= 10) AND (A[LOC] <> KEY) DO LOC := LOC + 1
```

The error here is that if KEY is not in the array, the variable LOC will eventually be set to the array size plus one (in this case, 11). One might expect that the WHILE loop would then quit, because (LOC <= N) is then FALSE; but the entire condition is evaluated, getting FALSE for this part but then attempting to evaluate (A[LOC] <> KEY) to AND with it. Since LOC = 11 is not a valid subscript for A, an array subscripting error occurs.

This problem does not occur in languages that do not check your array subscripts—but Pascal does, because an array subscript out of bounds can cause some really mysterious errors to occur (as you probably already know). If the subscript checking causes you trouble, there are two things you can do about it: (1) turn off the subscript checking, if your compiler has this option, or (2) program it correctly.

There is no input/output defined for entire arrays; they must be input or output element by element. For example, the following code outputs array A on a single line.

```
FOR I := 1 TO N DO WRITE (A[I]);
WRITELN
```

This code may or may not work if the resultant line is too long to print. Most installations have an absolute limit on how long a line may be, and it is an error to try to exceed that limit. Sometimes the limit is larger than may be printed on a single line, and in that case it is up to the particular output device to decide what to do with the excess. In short, this code is only good for small values of N.

If N could be large, and you could print at most K values per line, the code becomes more complex.

```
COUNT := 0;       (* number of items on current line *)
FOR  I := 1 TO N DO
       BEGIN
       WRITE (A[I]);
       COUNT := (COUNT + 1) MOD K;
       IF (COUNT = 0) OR (I = N) THEN WRITELN
       END
```

In this code COUNT takes on the values 0, 1, ..., $K - 1$, then cycles back to zero. Each time it is reset to zero, a WRITELN is performed to end the line. In addition, a WRITELN is performed after the last value of the array, regardless of its position on the line.

Recall that array B is dimensioned [1..M, 1..N]. The following code prints out B as M rows of N numbers each (assuming N numbers will fit on a single line).

```
FOR I := 1 TO M DO
       BEGIN
       FOR J := 1 TO N DO WRITE (B[I, J]);
       WRITELN
       END
```

To read in array B, no READLN is needed. Pascal automatically skips over end-of-line marks on input, so the code is simply

```
FOR I := 1 TO M DO
    FOR J := 1 TO N DO
        READ (B[I, J])
```

Chapter 11

CHARACTERS AND STRINGS

There is no data type "string" in Standard Pascal, but there is a data type CHAR for single characters; strings can be built as arrays of CHAR. UCSD Pascal does provide a type STRING.

11.1 CHARACTERS

A CHAR constant consists of a single character enclosed in single quote marks (apostrophes), for example,

'A'   '3'   '$'

The only exception to this rule is that the single quote character itself must be represented by two successive single quote marks enclosed in single quotes, giving four in all.

''''   represents the single quote character.

Characters may be assigned to variables, passed as parameters, compared for equality or inequality (see below), and input and output.

As always, characters are stored internally as small integers, according to a numeric code called the "collating sequence," which varies from one computer to the next. The collating sequence contains many invisible characters, such as linefeed, carriage return, rubout, bell, etc. To give you access to these characters, there are two standard functions.

CHR(*i*)   where *i* is a small integer, returns the character corresponding to that integer.

ORD(*c*)   where *c* is a character, returns the integer corresponding to that character.

If you wish to use these functions, you should try to obtain a table of the collating sequence used by your computer. Appendix C gives the collating sequences used by the Pascal implementations described in this book. Even if your implementation is not one of these, it may still use one of these collating sequences.

If you cannot get a copy of the collating sequence used by your computer, the following program may tell you the codes for visible characters, and may give you some clues about the invisible ones.

```
PROGRAM COLLSEQ(OUTPUT);
      (* Try to print the collating sequence. *)
VAR
      I: INTEGER;
BEGIN
      FOR I:=0 TO 255 DO WRITELN(I:5,' <',CHR(I),'>')
END.
```

This program can bomb in several ways (there may be fewer than 256 characters, or some of the characters might do strange things such as log you out), but it is a start.

The various equality and inequality tests (= , < , < = , > , > = , <>) can be applied to characters directly, and the result will be the same as you would get by comparing the ORDs of the characters. For example, the test (CH > = 'A') is equivalent to (ORD(CH) > = ORD('A')). The result in either case depends on the particular collating sequence used by your computer.

Two other functions defined on characters are also dependent on the particular collating sequence. They are

PRED(*ch*)   returns the character that precedes *ch* in the collating sequence, and is undefined if *ch* is the first character.

SUCC(*ch*)   returns the character which succeeds (follows) *ch* in the collating sequence, and is undefined if *ch* is the last character.

Normally you should avoid writing programs that depend on the collating sequence, because such programs are hard to read and are machine-dependent. One exception to this rule is converting from (character) digits to their integer values, and back again. Any sane collating sequence will assign consecutive codes to the digits '0'.. '9', in that order, hence the following code almost always works.

ORD(ch) $-$ ORD('0')   returns the numeric value (0..9) of the digit ch ('0'.. '9').

CHR(n + ORD('0'))   returns the character ('0'.. '9') corresponding to the integer n, where $0 <= n <= 9$.

Characters may be input and output. On output, each character normally occupies a single print position, that is, no extra blanks are output. When a field width is explicitly given, as in WRITE(CH:6), the character is right justified in the field, preceded by blanks.

On input, blanks are not skipped over—they too are characters. A newline, that is, an end-of-line marker, is read in as a single blank. (This is true even when your system uses more than one character to mark the end of a line, such as carriage return/linefeed.)

To distinguish a true blank from a newline masquerading as a blank, use the function EOLN(*filename*); the *filename* may be omitted, in which case INPUT is assumed. EOLN returns TRUE when the last character before the line terminator has just been read, that is, when the blank representing a newline is next in line to be read. Hence, to read an entire line, use

```
VAR
    S: ARRAY [1..100] OF CHAR;
    N: INTEGER;
. . .
N:=0;
WHILE NOT EOLN DO        (* while another char do *)
    BEGIN
    N:=N+1;              (*     read it *)
    READ(S[N])
    END;
READLN;                  (* skip over newline *)
(* N is the number of characters read *)
```

11.2 STRINGS, EXCEPT IN UCSD PASCAL

(If you are using UCSD Pascal, this section does not apply to you. Read Section 11.3 instead.)

Strings in Pascal are implemented in a rather half-hearted way. There is really no such type as a string, but there are string constants. A string constant consists of two or more characters enclosed in single quote marks, for example, 'HELLO'. A single character enclosed in quotes is not a string but a CHAR. There is no provision for a null string (a string containing no characters at all). If you desire to have a single quote inside a string constant, it must be written twice. 'DON''T GO' contains eight characters, while ' '''''' contains two.

In Standard Pascal, a string constant is regarded as a value of type PACKED ARRAY [1..*n*] OF CHAR, where *n* is the length of (number of characters in) the string. The keyword PACKED indicates to the compiler that storage usage is to be minimized (usually by storing more than one character per word).

Pascal allows assignment of one entire array to another, provided that their types are identical. This facility also works for strings; but the length of a string is an essential part of its type, so the lengths of the strings must be equal. For example, given the declarations

```
VAR
     S: PACKED ARRAY [1..4] OF CHAR;
     C: PACKED ARRAY [1..1] OF CHAR;
```

the following assignments are legal:

```
S := 'BOAT';
S := 'CAR ';
S := ' CAR';
```

but the following assignments are illegal:

```
S := 'HOUSE';      (* types don't match *)
S := 'CAR';        (* types don't match *)
C := 'X';          (* types don't match—'X' is a CHAR *)
```

As a bonus, Pascal allows you to output constant strings, but it does not extend this courtesy to arrays. Hence

```
WRITE('BOAT')      is legal, but
WRITE(S)           is not legal
```

Pascal 8000 is extended to provide input/output for any PACKED ARRAY [1..*n*] OF CHAR.

Several versions of Pascal have a predefined type ALFA. In Pascal 8000 ALFA is defined as PACKED ARRAY (. 1..8 .) OF CHAR (and can be input/output). In CDC Pascal type ALFA is defined as PACKED ARRAY [1..10] OF CHAR; output is defined for ALFA variables, but not input.

Packed strings of the same length may also be compared for equality and inequality with the operators =, <, <=, >, >=, and <>. Comparisons are lexicographic, that is, the leftmost characters are compared first, then the next leftmost, and so forth. The result is almost an alphabetical ordering on strings, depending on the collating sequence; however, if the blank comes after the letters in the collating sequence, that is, if ORD(' ') > ORD('A'), then short words will be larger than long ones, for example, 'AT ' > 'ATE'.

In all other respects, strings behave as ordinary packed arrays, and most of the things you would do with strings you can do by manipulating individual array elements. For example, the following program reads in a fixed-length string and tests whether it is a palindrome.

```
PROGRAM PALINDROME(INPUT, OUTPUT);
      (* Test if input string is a palindrome *)
CONST
      STRINGSIZE = 10;
VAR
      S, T: PACKED ARRAY [1..STRINGSIZE] OF CHAR;
      I: INTEGER;
      CH: CHAR;

BEGIN
FOR I:=1 TO STRINGSIZE DO
      BEGIN   (* read in string *)
      READ(CH); S[I]:=CH
      END;
FOR I:=1 TO STRINGSIZE DO
      T[STRINGSIZE+1-I]:=S[I];        (* T:=reverse(S) *)
WRITE(' STRING IS');
IF S<>T THEN WRITE(' NOT');
WRITELN(' A PALINDROME.')
END.
```

It is occasionally desirable to represent a string as a normal (unpacked) array of characters. Each representation has its advantages and disadvantages.

Normal Array	Packed Array
Faster access to individual elements.	Consumes less storage.
Can pass individual elements as parameters.	Can use string constants and the tests $=$, $<$, $<=$, $>$, $>=$, $<>$.
Can input/output individual elements.	On some implementations, can input/output entire strings.

Individual elements of a packed array may not be used as VAR parameters. Since READ, WRITE, and their variations are considered to be procedure calls, individual elements of packed arrays cannot be input. This restriction is easy to get around by means of temporary variables; see the use of CH in the above palindrome program for an example.

To facilitate the packing and unpacking of arrays, two standard functions are provided. They are somewhat confusing, so are seldom used; you can do the same things with simple loops, assigning the individual elements of one array to the other.

PACK(*na, i, pa*)   where *na* is a normal array and *pa* is a packed array, will completely fill *pa* with characters from *na* beginning at location *na*[*i*].

UNPACK(*pa*, *i*, *na*)   will copy into *na*, starting at *na*[*i*], all the characters from *pa*.

For normal use *na* and *pa* would be dimensioned the same, with *i* set to the lowest subscript (usually 1). Otherwise, note that

• The array being copied from is always given first.
• *i* always refers to the starting location in the unpacked array.
• The number of characters moved is always based on the the total length of the packed array.
• An error may result from exceeding the bounds of either array.

PACK and UNPACK can be applied to packed and unpacked arrays of any type, not just arrays of CHAR.

PASLC requires a fourth parameter to both PACK and UNPACK which explicitly specifies the number of array elements to be moved.

11.3   STRINGS IN UCSD PASCAL

A declaration of a STRING in UCSD Pascal may have either of two forms

STRING [*maxlength*]

in which *maxlength* is the maximum number of characters that can be in the string (up to a limit of 255), and

STRING

in which *maxlength* is assumed to be 80. For example,

VAR
      NAME, ADDRESS: STRING;
      STANZA: STRING[255];

A string constant consists of zero or more characters inside single quote marks, for example, ' ', 'A', ' ''#$%', 'DON''T GO'. As in Standard Pascal, a single quote mark can be represented inside a string constant by writing it twice. String constants may not contain the newline character, so you cannot start a string on one line and continue it on the next.

A CHAR is not the same thing as a string containing only one character; however, a constant of exactly one character (for example, 'A') may represent either a CHAR or a STRING, and UCSD Pascal will usually figure out which type is intended. In a procedure or function call such a constant is always assumed to be of type CHAR, and this may lead to syntax errors.

In UCSD Pascal you may declare a type PACKED ARRAY [1..*length*] OF CHAR, but this is different from a STRING, and cannot be used like one.

Strings may be assigned values and may be compared to one another with the comparison operators =, <>, >, >=, <, and <=. The comparison is lexicographical, that is, one string is less than another if it precedes it alphabetically. In ASCII, the blank has a lower value than any letter, hence causes no trouble; but all lowercase characters have larger values than all uppercase characters, so you must convert to a single case before you attempt to alphabetize strings.

String lengths vary dynamically. The length of a string is the number of characters in its present value, so that after assigning 'HELLO' to string S, S will have length 5. Strings may be assigned, compared, and passed as parameters, regardless of their current lengths.

Strings may be indexed; S[1] is the first character of string S. It is an error to index beyond the current length of the string, so for instance if S has the value 'HELLO', it would be illegal to refer to S[6]. This error can be surprisingly difficult to avoid.

You cannot define a function which returns a STRING as its value, but UCSD Pascal provides several such functions. They are

CONCAT (*string1* , *string2* , ..., *stringN*)

> Returns a string that is the concatenation (putting together) of its parameters. For example, CONCAT('HOT', 'DOG', 'S') returns 'HOTDOGS'.

COPY (*string* , *start_position* , *length*)

> Returns the substring of length *length* starting at position *start_position* of *string* (same as MID$ in Basic). For example, COPY('GANDER', 2, 3) returns 'AND'.

LENGTH (*string*)

> Returns the current length of *string*. For example, LENGTH('HELLO') returns 5.

POS (*string1* , *string2*)

> Searches for *string1* as a substring of *string2*, and returns its starting position if found, or zero if not found. For example, POS('WRITE', 'IT') returns 3.

UCSD Pascal also provides three procedures which modify their parameters. They are

DELETE (*string* , *start_position* , *length*)

> Modifies the given *string* by deleting *length* characters from it, starting at *start_position*. For example, if S has the value 'READ', then the call DELETE(S, 3, 1) will change S to 'RED'.

INSERT (*insertion* , *string* , *position*)

> Modifies *string* by inserting the *insertion* (also a string) in the given *position*. For example, if S has the value 'RED', it can be changed to 'READ' by the call INSERT('A', S, 3).

STR (*integer* , *string*)

> Assigns to the *string* a sequence of characters representing the numeric value of the *integer*. For instance, STR(100, S) would assign '100' to string S. STR may also be used with long integers.

The following example illustrates the most common problems you will have in working with strings. Suppose you want to test whether the first character of string S1 occurs in string S2. You might write

```
IF POS(S1[1], S2) > 0 THEN ...        (* error *)
```

but this would be wrong because S1[1] is a CHAR and POS expects a STRING. To fix this error you could declare a third STRING S3 and try

```
S3 := S1[1];        (* error *)
IF POS(S3, S2) > 0 THEN ...
```

This is wrong because S3 and S1[1] are of different types. Next you might try

```
S3[1] := S1[1];        (* possible error *)
IF POS(S3, S2) > 0 THEN ...        (* possible error *)
```

The syntax is now correct but the code is still wrong. The assignment is illegal if S3 is initially the empty string (the string containing zero characters) because S3[1] is beyond the current length of that string. If S3 is longer than one character, then only its first character is changed; the code will run and search S2 for the wrong thing.

The correct code for this problem is

```
S3:= '?';        (* to make S3 a string of length 1 *)
S3[1]:= S1[1];
IF POS(S3, S2) > 0 THEN ...
```

With experience in string handling you can often find simpler ways to do things. In the above example S1[1] gave us trouble because it is of type CHAR; but COPY(S1, 1, 1) is the same as S1[1] except that COPY always returns a STRING. This observation yields a simpler solution.

```
IF POS(COPY(S1, 1, 1), S2) > 0 THEN ...
```

Strings may be output with either WRITE or WRITELN. Strings may be input with either READ or READLN, and in either case the value read in consists of all the characters remaining on the input line, up to but not including the newline character. READLN is generally preferable to READ because it also reads and discards the newline character that marks the end of the input string.

Chapter 12

RECORDS AND POINTERS

In COBOL, records are used to group data and to specify storage layout, generally for I/O purposes. In Pascal, records are not so closely associated with I/O (in fact, record I/O for textfiles is not defined), but are used to group data and to give some measure of control over storage layout.

Records and pointers are used together primarily to create new data structures such as linked lists. This chapter will give you the tools to build such data structures.

If you have worked with linked lists before, you already understand their uses, and will easily learn to use records and pointers. If not, your main problem will be not so much learning how to use records and pointers, but discovering what they are good for. Careful perusal of the examples should help some; beyond that, you should consider acquiring a good book on data structures.

12.1 SIMPLE GROUPING

Records provide a means of grouping data items of possibly different types. Records may be either "fixed" or "variant," and these two kinds of records have different uses. The fixed record is simpler and will be described first; its syntax is

```
RECORD
      list_of_field_names_1 : type;
      list_of_field_names_2 : type;
      . . .
```

```
        list_of_field_names_n : type          (* no semicolon *)
END
```

where each *field_name* is a distinct identifier, and a *list_of_field_names* consists of one or more field names separated by commas. Thus we can, for example, declare a new type FRACTION as

```
TYPE
    FRACTION = RECORD
        NUM, DENOM: INTEGER
    END
```

This describes, or provides a blueprint for, objects of the new type FRACTION, but does not itself create any variables of this type. Allocating variables of type FRACTION is done in the VAR section, as follows.

```
VAR
    A, B, C: FRACTION
```

Each variable of type FRACTION is a record containing two fields, NUM and DENOM. The variables A, B, and C may be treated as simple variables for purposes of parameter transmission, assignment, or tests of exact equality, for example,

```
C:=A;
IF A = B THEN ...;
```

However, neither input/output (for textfiles) nor any of the ordering relations ($<$, $<=$, $>$, $>=$) is defined for records.

Standard Pascal does not allow record constants. Pascal 8000 does provide record constants, of the form

```
(# value_1, value_2, ..., value_n #)
```

where there must be the same number of *values* as fields in the record, and the values must be of the types required by the corresponding fields.

For example, to set fraction A to the value 3/4, one may write (in Pascal 8000 only)

```
A := (# 3, 4 #)
```

Many operations must be described in terms of the individual fields of particular record variables. NUM and DENOM are not themselves the names of variables, and may not be used independently of the particular record variable in which they occur. The syntax used to refer to a particular field of a particular record is

```
record_name . field_name
```

so that to double the numerator of fraction A, one would write

A.NUM := 2∗A.NUM

As a second example, the rule for adding two fractions in elementary arithmetic is

$$\frac{u}{v} + \frac{x}{y} = \frac{uy + vx}{vy} \; ;$$

To add the Pascal fractions A (representing u/v) and B (representing x/y) to get the sum in C, one would write

C.NUM := A.NUM∗B.DENOM + A.DENOM∗B.NUM;
C.DENOM := A.DENOM∗B.DENOM

and to output this result,

WRITELN(' SUM =', C.NUM, '/', C.DENOM)

Records may be used wherever it is desirable to group related data values into a single unit, as in the case of a fraction. There are two other common uses of records: to build linked data structures, and to deal with data items whose type is not known in advance. For the former, we need pointer types; for the latter, variant records.

12.2 POINTERS

A "pointer" is a variable that refers to another variable of a specified type. For example, we may have a "pointer to real," which can refer only to some real variable. The syntax of a pointer declaration is

↑ *type*

where type is the type of variable pointed to. In practice, 99% of the pointers used refer to one kind or another of record.

Consider the problem of building a linked list. The individual nodes of the linked list will each contain some value (say, an integer), and will also refer to the next node in the list. The following does not work

```
TYPE
    NODE = RECORD
            VAL: INTEGER;
            NEXT: NODE      (∗ illegal ∗)
    END
```

because a NODE is not big enough to contain another whole NODE inside it (which in turn contains another node, *ad infinitum*). This definition leads to an infinitely large structure.

A pointer to a node, however, is of a fixed size, and may occur as a component of a node, for example,

```
TYPE
    NODE = RECORD
            VAL: INTEGER
            NEXT: ↑NODE
    END
```

This definition allows us to build linked lists of NODEs.

In Pascal, a name must be declared prior to any use of that name. An exception is made for pointers, so that we may use ↑NODE before (or during) the declaration of NODE, as we have just done above. In this case, a NODE must still be declared somewhere within the current section of declarations.

There is a special pointer value NIL which can be assigned to any pointer of any type; it has the interpretation "undefined," or "this pointer does not point to anything." It is used to indicate a missing pointer, as at the end of a linked list.

Pointers have a very limited set of operations defined on them. Assume the declarations

```
VAR
    P, Q: ↑T;
    N: ↑NODE
```

for some types T and NODE; then the allowable operations on pointers are

1 Assignment. P: = Q causes P to point to the same object (of type T) as Q points to. The assignment P: = N is not legal because P and N are of different types.

2 Test for equality. The comparisons P = Q and P<>Q are allowed. P and N are of different types and cannot be compared, nor are the inequality tests P>Q, P> = Q, P<Q, P< = Q allowed.

3 Following the pointer. The notation P↑ indicates the variable (of type T) to which P points. Any operations defined for type T may be applied to P↑; for example, if T is a NODE (as defined above), then it is legal to refer to its fields P↑.VAL and P↑.NEXT. Note, however, that if P is NIL, then P↑ is illegal (you cannot follow a missing pointer).

4 Creation of a new object. The procedure call NEW(P) creates a new object of type T, and makes P point to it. This is especially useful in creating linked structures. (The procedure NEW can take additional parameters; see Section 12.7 for details.)

5 Deletion of a previously created object. The procedure call DIS-

POSE(P) gets rid of the object pointed to by P. The storage space used is thus recycled. (In many versions of Pascal, DISPOSE is not implemented; see Section 12.7.)

It is important to note certain operations that cannot be done with pointers. In general, these are not allowed because they are unsafe operations.

1 Given only an object X of type T and a pointer P of type $\uparrow$T, it is impossible to make P point to X. The only way to create a pointer value is by use of the procedure NEW(P), which creates another object of that type and makes P point to the new object; but you cannot create a pointer to an already existing object. Once you have a pointer to an object, however, you can make as many copies of that pointer as you like, by assignment.

2 Arithmetic cannot be performed on pointers.

3 The inequality tests $>$, $> =$, $<$, $< =$ cannot be performed on pointers, because it is supposed to be conceptually meaningless. This fiction may not be maintained in newer versions of Pascal.

4 Input and output are not defined for pointers. Nonetheless, some Pascal implementations may allow you to print out pointer values (as octal or hex numbers) for debugging purposes.

12.3   EXAMPLE: STACK OPERATIONS

Suppose you have a stack of books, and that you can see or move only one book at the time. This limits the number of things you can do with that stack. You can (1) see if the stack is empty, (2) see what the top book on the stack is, (3) get the top book from the stack, or (4) put another book on the stack, on top of the books already there.

This leads to the abstract notion of a stack. A stack is a data structure with a limited number of operations defined on it, as follows.

1 You can see if a stack is EMPTY.

2 If a stack is not empty, you can LOOK at the top thing on the stack.

3 If a stack is not empty, you can remove (POP) the top thing from the stack.

4 You can put (PUSH) a new thing onto a stack.

In this example we implement a stack as a linked list. To be explicit, we shall implement a stack of integers, since Pascal always requires that we know the types of the variables we use. The first element of this list will serve as the top of the stack.

We begin with some declarations. Since the stack is to be a linked list, we define a record (which we shall call a "NODE") with two fields, "VAL" and "NEXT." The VAL field will hold the integer and the NEXT field will hold a pointer to the next node in the linked list.

Conceptually, we would like to refer to the entire linked list as a STACK, but there is no way to do this. We do need a pointer to the first element of the linked list, and we can give the type name STACK to this pointer. In practice, it seems to work well to name a pointer to a structure as if it were actually the structure itself.

```
TYPE
    NODE = RECORD
           VAL: INTEGER;
           NEXT: ↑NODE
    END;
    STACK = ↑NODE;
```

This describes the structure we will use in implementing stacks, but we do not yet have any instances of stacks. To make some stacks, (say, two of them), we need to declare them in the VAR section.

```
VAR
    S1, S2: STACK;
```

Now we proceed to define operations on stacks.

```
FUNCTION EMPTY(S: STACK): BOOLEAN;
    (* return TRUE if stack S is empty, else return FALSE *)
    BEGIN
        EMPTY := (S = NIL)
    END;


FUNCTION LOOK(S: STACK): INTEGER;
    (* return the value of the top element on stack S *)
    BEGIN
        IF EMPTY(S) THEN
            WRITELN(
            ' ERROR: FUNCTION "LOOK" GIVEN EMPTY STACK.')
        ELSE
            LOOK := S↑.VAL
    END;
```

Here S is actually a pointer to the first NODE in the stack, S↑ is that first node, and S↑.VAL is the integer part of the node.

```
PROCEDURE POP(VAR S: STACK);
    (* delete the top element from stack S *)
    BEGIN      (* See Figure 12.1 *)
        IF EMPTY(S) THEN
```

```
            WRITELN(
              ' ERROR: PROCEDURE "POP" GIVEN EMPTY  STACK')
        ELSE
              S := S↑.NEXT      (* See Figure 12.2 *)
    END;
```

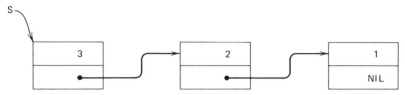

Fig. 12.1 Stack S before the POP operation, assuming that S contains the values 3 (at the top of the stack), 2, and 1 (at the bottom of the stack). The VAL field is shown as the top half of each box, and the NEXT field is shown as the bottom half.

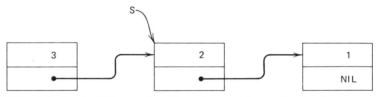

Fig. 12.2 Stack S after the POP operation. The node containing 3 still exists, but is unreachable; 2 is now at the top of the stack.

POP works by simply moving the pointer S past the first element of S. The first element then becomes inaccessible. If memory is scarce, so that recycling waste memory is necessary, then the following code is appropriate.

```
PROCEDURE POP(VAR S: STACK);       (* alternate version *)
    (* delete and recycle the top element from stack S *)
    VAR
        TEMP: STACK;
    BEGIN
        IF EMPTY(S) THEN
            WRITELN(
              ' ERROR: PROCEDURE "POP" GIVEN EMPTY STACK.')
        ELSE
            BEGIN
            TEMP := S;             (* remember old top element *)
            S := S↑.NEXT;          (* step S past top element *)
            DISPOSE(TEMP)          (* recycle old top element *)
            END
    END;
```

The ordering of operations here is critical. We must get the information we need (S↑.NEXT) out of the first node before we dispose of it; but we cannot set S to S↑.NEXT first, because then we lose track of the record to be recycled. Hence, a temporary variable is necessary to retain this information.

```
PROCEDURE PUSH(ITEM: INTEGER; VAR S: STACK);
        (* put the ITEM on the top of stack S *)
        VAR
            TEMP: ↑NOTE;
    BEGIN                      (* See Figure 12.3 *)
        NEW(TEMP);             (* See Figure 12.4 *)
        TEMP↑.VAL := ITEM;     (* See Figure 12.5 *)
        TEMP↑.NEXT := S;       (* See Figure 12.6 *)
        S := TEMP              (* See Figure 12.7 *)
    END;
```

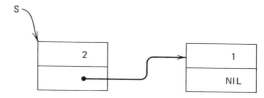

Fig. 12.3 Stack S before the PUSH(3, S) operation, assuming that S contains the values 2 (at the stack top) and 1.

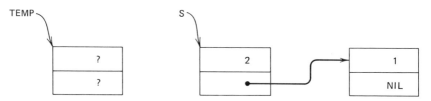

Fig. 12.4 Stack S after executing the call NEW(TEMP) . A new code has been gotten, but not yet attached to the rest of the stack; its fields may contain garbage.

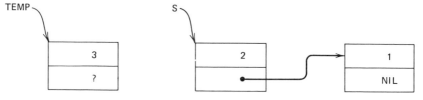

Fig. 12.5 Stack S after executing the statement TEMP↑.VAL := ITEM , assuming that ITEM was given the value 3 by the call to PUSH.

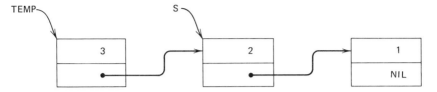

Fig. 12.6 Stack S after executing the statement TEMP↑.NEXT := S . The new node has been attached to the rest of the stack, but is not yet reachable from pointer S.

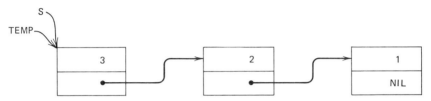

Fig. 12.7 Stack S after executing the statement S := TEMP . The node containing 3 is now at the top of stack S; variable TEMP is local to procedure PUSH, and will disappear when PUSH returns.

Note that PUSH and both versions of POP work by altering the value of S, the pointer to the stack. Hence S must be declared as a VAR parameter.

Although not a standard stack operation, we introduce an additional procedure DUMPSTACK to print the entire contents of a stack. DUMP-STACK may be useful in debugging; it also illustrates the general technique of stepping through a linked list.

```
PROCEDURE DUMPSTACK(S: STACK);
      (* print out the contents of stack S *)
      VAR
            HERE: ↑NODE;
      BEGIN
            IF S = NIL THEN
                  WRITELN(' STACK IS EMPTY.')
            ELSE
                  BEGIN
                  HERE := S;
                  WRITELN (' (TOP OF STACK)');
                  WHILE HERE <> NIL DO
                        BEGIN
                        WRITELN('       ', HERE↑.VAL);
                        HERE := HERE↑.NEXT
                        END
                  END
      END;
```

HERE is a local variable that is initialized to point to the first element of the list, and that "walks along" the list. The assignment HERE: = HERE ↑ .NEXT steps HERE to point to the next node in sequence.

One final caution is in order. We have defined two stacks, S1 and S2, but they have not yet been initialized and may contain garbage. Attempting to use a pointer that contains garbage can result in almost anything. Be safe and initialize them before you do anything else, by

```
S1 := NIL;
S2 := NIL;
```

Now the stacks are ready for use.

12.4 VARIANT RECORDS

Variant records provide a means of unifying records that are similar but not identical in form, and also make it possible to circumvent the type-checking mechanism. We will consider each of these uses in turn.

Suppose you are building a bibliography. Some of your entries are books, others are journal articles. You need to maintain somewhat different information in each case, such as

Book: Author(s), title, date, publisher, city.
Article: Author(s), title, date, journal, volume, number, pages.

You could define two different kinds of records, BOOK and ARTICLE, but then these would be of different types and you could not mix them in a single array or a single linked list.

You could define one kind of record with all of the above fields, and just use the fields you need for each particular entry. This wastes storage, and the unused fields are esthetically displeasing.

The Pascal solution is to provide a structure called a "variant record." A variant record is a record with an (optional) "fixed" part, which has the same fields for all records of that type, and a "variant" part, which has one of a predefined set of groups of fields. A "tag field" is also generally included, to specify which variant part is currently in use.

A somewhat simplified syntax is

```
RECORD
     fixed_part;
     CASE tag : type_identifier OF
          case_label_list : ( field_list ) ;
          . . .
          case_label_list : ( field_list )        (* No ";" *)
END
```

where *fixed_part* is the same as in a fixed record, that is, it stands for

list_of_field_names_1 : *type* ;
list_of_field_names_2 : *type* ;
. . .
list_of_field_names_n : *type*

tag is the name of a field used to indicate dynamically (during execution) which variant is currently in use.

type_identifier is the name of the type of *tag*. It must be a type name, not a type description.

case_label_list is a list of one or more values, separated by commas, which may be taken on by the *tag*.

Notice that one END ends the entire variant record construct. The CASE part does not have a separate END, as you might expect by analogy with a CASE statement.

It may be helpful to consider an example before going into more detail.

```
TYPE
      SOURCE = (BOOK, ARTICLE);
      SHORTSTRING = PACKED ARRAY [1..20] OF CHAR;
      LONGSTRING = PACKED ARRAY [1..50] OF CHAR;
      AUTHORLIST = RECORD
            AUTHOR: SHORTSTRING;
            NEXTAUTHOR: ↑AUTHORLIST
      END;
      BIBENTRY = RECORD
            AUTHORS: AUTHORLIST;
            TITLE: LONGSTRING;
            DATE: 1900..2000;
            CASE SOURCETAG: SOURCE OF
                  BOOK:
                        (PUBLISHER, CITY: SHORTSTRING);
                  ARTICLE:
                        (JOURNAL: LONGSTRING;
                        VOLUME, NUMBER, FIRSTPAGE, LASTPAGE:
                        INTEGER)
      END;
      BIBLIOGRAPHY: ARRAY[1..500] OF BIBENTRY;
VAR
      COMPUTERS, PSYCHOLOGY, HISTORY: BIBLIOGRAPHY;
```

Now any BIBENTRY (say for example COMPUTERS[25]) may represent either a BOOK with six fields or an ARTICLE with nine. You set the tag field, COMPUTERS[25].SOURCETAG, to tell which it is; later you can look at this field to find out which it is. If you want to change the entry later, you may change the tag field just as you would any other field. However, it is your responsibility to change the fields in the variant part to correspond to the new tag value.

The storage used by BIBENTRY may be interpreted in either of two ways, corresponding to the two possible values of SOURCETAG (see Fig. 12.8). Enough storage is allocated for the largest possible variant, so that some storage will be wasted when shorter variants are in use (such as when SOURCETAG = BOOK in the current example), but the problem is not severe.

The fields of the fixed part have the same meaning, regardless of the current value of its SOURCETAG. The storage following the SOURCETAG has a dual purpose: it can be used for the fields unique to BOOKs, or for the fields unique to ARTICLEs, but not for both simultaneously. If you execute the pair of statements

```
COMPUTERS[1].JOURNAL := THISJOURNAL;
COMPUTERS[1].CITY := THISCITY;
```

then the information stored by the second assignment would destroy part of the information stored by the first.

To avoid this situation, you should always check the tag field to make sure it is correct before you use the variant fields. Pascal does not automatically perform this check for you.

If you do not need the *tag* field, you may omit it. (Usually this occurs when you have some other way of knowing which variant you are using.) In this case you leave out the *tag*, and the colon which follows it, but you must still have a *type_identifier* so that Pascal knows what kind of *field_names* to expect.

```
TYPE
    BIBENTRY = RECORD
        . . .
        CASE SOURCE OF
            . . .
    END
```

The compiler uses the type information, but no space is allocated in the variant record for a value of that type.

A variant record without a tag field can be used to access specific addresses in memory. We set up the record so that an integer and a pointer share the same storage location; then, by setting the integer component to any desired address, we effectively make the pointer point to that address.

```
TYPE
    BYTE = 0..255;
        FLEXPOINTER = RECORD
            CASE BOOLEAN OF
                TRUE: (ADDR: INTEGER);
```

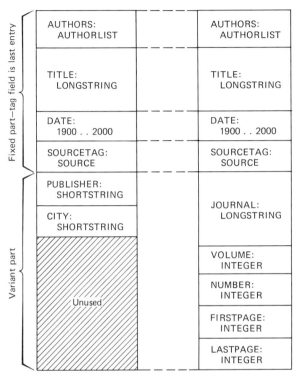

Fig. 12.8 The two ways that the storage used by a BIBENTRY may be interpreted. The case SOURCETAG = BOOK is shown on the left, and SOURCETAG = ARTICLE on the right.

```
              FALSE: (PTR: ↑BYTE)
    END;
```

This declaration assumes a byte-oriented machine (that is, every character location has an address). On a word-oriented machine we could use ↑INTEGER instead of ↑BYTE, since an integer usually occupies one word of storage.

The following routines to fetch from and store in specific machine locations are modeled after BASIC.

```
PROCEDURE POKE(ADR: INTEGER; VAL: BYTE);
    (* Store value VAL at location ADR *)
    VAR
        MEM: FLEXPOINTER;
    BEGIN
        MEM.ADDR := ADR;
        MEM.PTR↑ := VAL
    END;
```

```
FUNCTION PEEK(ADR: INTEGER): BYTE;
    (* Return the value in location ADR *)
    VAR
        MEM: FLEXPOINTER;
    BEGIN
        MEM.ADDR := ADR;
        PEEK := MEM.PTR ↑
    END;
```

This technique works well for most ordinary memory locations. However, many computers have specific machine addresses which perform some function (such as changing the mode of the display) whenever they are accessed, regardless of whether the value at that address has been changed. This can be a problem in UCSD Pascal because in that system all accesses are to "words," which are consecutive pairs of bytes. Only the byte you PEEK or POKE is affected by the call, but access is always made to an adjacent byte as well, sometimes with unexpected results. Probably the best solution to this problem is to recode PEEK and POKE in assembly language.

Finally, you may have variant parts within variant parts. The syntax is as you would expect, but remember that the fixed part always precedes the variant part, and that the CASE does not have an associated END.

Example:

```
TYPE
    SHAPE = (TRIANGLE, QUADRILATERAL);
    QUADSHAPE = (SQUARE, RHOMBUS);
    OBJECT = RECORD
        AREA: REAL;
        XCOORD, YCOORD: INTEGER;
        CASE SHAPE OF        (* tag field omitted *)
            TRIANGLE:
                (SIDE1, SIDE2: REAL;
                ANGLE: 1..79);
            QUADRILATERAL:
                (WIDTH: REAL;
                CASE Q: QUADSHAPE OF
                    SQUARE: ( );        (* null field *)
                    RHOMBUS: (ANGL: 1..179) )
    END
```

Standard Pascal allows records to have null fields (such as the field labeled by SQUARE) in both the fixed and the variant parts. UCSD Pascal does not permit null fields in records.

12.5   EXAMPLE: LEXICAL SCANNING

Pascal input is satisfactory when the type of the next input item is known in advance. In many nonnumeric applications, however, it is necessary to read the next input item and then to determine its type. A program to do this kind of input is called a "lexical scanner."

A lexical scanner works by reading the input character-by-character, and putting the characters together into meaningful groups. The value thus computed may be any of a number of types; one way to return the value to the calling program is by means of a variant record, which can hold any one of the possible types.

The following lexical scanner reads only three types: integers, variable names (consisting of a letter followed by zero or more letters and digits), and special characters. It could readily be extended to handle real numbers. The lexical scanner READSYMBOL is shown embedded in a complete program, in order to show the declarations needed and to give an example of its use.

To use the scanner, include the CONST and TYPE declarations in your program as shown (you may change the STRGSIZE if you like). Then declare at least one variable of type SYMBOL, such as S in the example program. To call the scanner, do

```
READSYMBOL(S)
```

and the next "symbol" (integer, string, or single character) will be returned in S.

To use the symbol thus returned, you must first check the value of S.FLAG (which is of type INDICATOR).

If S.FLAG is	you can use	which is of type
NUMBER	S.INT	INTEGER
VARIABLE	S.STR	STRG
PUNCTUATION	S.CH	CHAR

The sample program uses a CASE statement to decide, on the basis of S.FLAG, which of S.INT, S.STR, or S.CH it is legal to use. Since these are variant fields of a record, only one of them may be in use at a time.

One problem with records in Pascal, particularly variant records, shows up quite clearly in this example. The problem is that it is often necessary to think up several different names for essentially the same thing.

Suppose, for example, that the lexical scanner reads an integer. This is indicated by setting the FLAG of the variant record to NUMBER, and saving the integer in the INT field. Both NUMBER and INT are used to mean INTEGER, but Pascal syntax requires different names for these two things. There is no easy solution to this problem; just learn to live with it.

```
PROGRAM LEX (INPUT, OUTPUT);

CONST
      STRGSIZE = 12;

TYPE
      STRG = PACKED ARRAY [1..STRGSIZE] OF CHAR;
      INDICATOR = (NUMBER, VARIABLE, PUNCTUATION);
      SYMBOL = RECORD
            CASE FLAG: INDICATOR OF
                  NUMBER: (INT: INTEGER);
                  VARIABLE: (STR: STRG);
                  PUNCTUATION: (CH: CHAR)
            END;

VAR
      S:    SYMBOL;
      I:    INTEGER;
      DONE: BOOLEAN;


(* -------- Lexical scanner starts here -------- *)

PROCEDURE READSYMBOL(VAR S: SYMBOL);
      (* This procedure reads one SYMBOL from input, where SYMBOL is
      either an unsigned integer, a variable name, or a single nonblank,
      nonalphanumeric character. The tag field of S is set to NUMBER,
      VARIABLE, or PUNCTUATION, respectively, and the corresponding
      data field is set accordingly. End-of-line indications are ignored. *)

      VAR
            I: INTEGER;

      FUNCTION LETTER(CH: CHAR): BOOLEAN;
      (* Return TRUE if CH is a letter, else return FALSE. This function does
      not work perfectly on IBM machines because EBCDIC has gaps in the
      collating sequence. *)
      BEGIN
            LETTER:= (CH >= 'A') AND (CH <= 'Z')
      END (* LETTER *);

FUNCTION DIGIT(CH: CHAR): BOOLEAN;
      (* Return TRUE if CH is a digit, else return FALSE *)
      BEGIN
            DIGIT:= (CH >= '0') AND (CH <= '9')
      END (* DIGIT *);
```

```
BEGIN (* READSYMBOL *)
WHILE INPUT↑ = ' ' DO GET(INPUT);          (* Skip blanks *)
IF DIGIT(INPUT↑) THEN (* Build integer *)
    BEGIN
    S.FLAG:=NUMBER;
    S.INT:=0;
    WHILE DIGIT(INPUT↑) DO
        BEGIN
        S.INT:=10*S.INT+ORD(INPUT↑)-ORD('0');
        GET(INPUT)
        END
     END
ELSE IF LETTER(INPUT↑) THEN (* Pack string *)
    BEGIN
    S.FLAG:=VARIABLE;
    I:=0;
    WHILE LETTER(INPUT↑) OR DIGIT(INPUT↑) DO
        BEGIN
        I:=I+1;
        IF I <= STRGSIZE THEN S.STR[I]:=INPUT↑;
        GET(INPUT)
        END;
    WHILE I < STRGSIZE DO (* Pad rest of string with blanks *)
        BEGIN
        I:=I+1;
        S.STR[I]:= ' '
        END
    END
ELSE (* Return as a single character *)
    BEGIN
    S.FLAG:=PUNCTUATION;
    S.CH:=INPUT↑;
    GET(INPUT)
    END
END (* GETSYMBOL *);



BEGIN (* -------- MAIN PROGRAM -------- *)
    (* Driver for procedure READSYMBOL *)
DONE:=FALSE;
REPEAT
    READSYMBOL(S);
    CASE S.FLAG OF
        NUMBER:
            WRITELN(' NUMBER:          ',S.INT);
```

```
            VARIABLE:
              BEGIN
              WRITE(' VARIABLE:           ');
              FOR I:=1 TO STRGSIZE DO WRITE(S.STR[I]);
              WRITELN;
              DONE:=(S.STR = 'END              ')   (* Exactly 9
              spaces *)
              END;
            PUNCTUATION:
              WRITELN(' PUNCTUATION:    ',S.CH)
      END
UNTIL DONE;
WRITELN(' Ehhh...that''s all, folks.')
END.
```

12.6   THE WITH STATEMENT

When doing several operations with the same record, it is sometimes cumbersome to keep repeating the name of that record. For example,

```
TYPE
      PERSON = RECORD
            NAME: PACKED ARRAY [1..30] OF CHAR;
            AGE: 18..65;
            WAGE: REAL
      END;
VAR
      EMPLOYEE: ARRAY [1..50] OF PERSON;
   . . .
WRITESTRG(EMPLOYEE[I].NAME);
EMPLOYEE[I].AGE:=EMPLOYEE[I].AGE+1;
WRITELN(' Age is ', EMPLOYEE[I].AGE);
EMPLOYEE[I].WAGE:=1.05*EMPLOYEE[I].WAGE;
WRITELN(' Wage is ', EMPLOYEE[I].WAGE);
IF EMPLOYEE[I].WAGE > MAXWAGE THEN FIRE(I)
```

The WITH statement provides a way to omit repetition of the record name. A simple form of the statement is

WITH *record* DO *statement*

Within the *statement* the fields of the *record* may be used as if they were simple variable names (this is sometimes called "opening the scope" of the record). Thus, the above example can be written more concisely as

```
WITH EMPLOYEE[I] DO
      BEGIN
```

```
WRITESTRG(NAME);
AGE: = AGE + 1;
WRITELN(' Age is ', AGE);
WAGE: = 1.05*WAGE;
WRITELN(' Wage is ', WAGE);
IF WAGE > MAXWAGE THEN FIRE(I)
END
```

Ordinary variables which are not field names of the specified record, such as MAXWAGE and I, may be used in the normal fashion inside the WITH statement.

While it is perfectly legal to change the values of the fields of the record named in the WITH statement, it is illegal to do anything which would result in the use of a different record. In the above example, it would be illegal to change the value of I inside the WITH statement, or to assign a different PERSON to EMPLOYEE[I].

The full syntax of the WITH statement is

WITH *record_1, record_2, ..., record_n* DO *statement*

which is equivalent to

WITH *record_1* DO
    WITH *record_2* DO
       . . .
          WITH *record_n* DO
            statement

12.7 ALLOCATING AND RECYCLING STORAGE

All versions of Pascal allow you to dynamically allocate storage by calling the procedure NEW. The simplest use of NEW is

NEW (*pointer_variable*)

where the parameter is a variable of type $\uparrow$T, for some type T. The effect is to allocate storage for a new variable of type T, and to make *pointer_value* point to this new variable.

For example, given the declarations

```
TYPE
    NODE = RECORD
        VAL: INTEGER;
        NEXT: ↑NODE
    END;
VAR
    HERE: ↑NODE
```

the call NEW(HERE) would create a new variable of type NODE (because HERE is of type pointer-to-NODE), and make HERE point to this new NODE.

NEW may be called with a pointer to a variant record type. In this case, enough storage is allocated for the largest possible variant of that type.

If you are pressed for storage space, and if when you ask for a NEW variant record you can guarantee that the tag fields of the variant parts will never be changed from their initial settings, then you can use a variation of NEW which will give you exactly the right amount of space for your particular variant,

NEW (*pointer_variable* , *tag1* , *tag2* , ..., *tagN*)

where you supply the *tag* values and NEW creates a variant record and sets the first parameter to point to it.

There may be multiple tags because the variant parts of records may themselves have variant parts. The tag values must be in order of increasing depth of nesting. If you stop before reaching the lowest level of nesting, enough space will be allocated for all possible values of the omitted tags. Oddly, NEW does not set the tag fields for you. You must set them to what you told NEW they would be, and you must not subsequently change them.

If you use this second form of NEW, you save storage but you lose a lot of rights. You can use the fields of the variant record as usual, but you cannot assign the whole record a value; you cannot use the whole record in an expression; and you cannot use it as an actual parameter.

Sometimes it happens that you no longer need some storage space that you had previously allocated and used. You may, if you wish, return this storage to the system for recycling. Such recycling happens automatically for local variables when the routine in which they are declared exits, but storage allocated by NEW is never automatically recycled. It is permanently allocated until you explicitly get rid of it.

The reason for permanent allocation is that it allows you to allocate storage within a routine and return that storage to the point of call. For example, the stack operations in Section 12.3 do exactly this: PUSH allocates a node and links it into a stack represented as a linked list. If this node were to disappear upon leaving PUSH, routines such as this would be impossible.

Recycling can be dangerous, however. If you recycle a piece of storage that you think you are through with, but which the program in fact will use again, you are in deep trouble. The Pascal system will likely not catch the error, and mysterious things will begin to happen. Therefore, if you can afford not to recycle, do not.

If there is a real danger that you may run out of storage, or if you are writing library routines for use by others, then you must recycle. There are two incompatible schemes for recycling storage. Standard Pascal, CDC Pascal, and UCSD Pascal V4 use DISPOSE, while UCSD Pascal, PASLC, and Pascal 8000 all use MARK/RELEASE.

DISPOSE is simple, allows fine control over what is to be recycled, and is the method defined by Standard Pascal. To recycle storage allocated by the first form of NEW, use

DISPOSE (*pointer_variable*)

and the thing pointed to by *pointer_variable* will be reclaimed by the system. (**Caution:** *pointer_variable* may still point to it.)

If the storage was allocated by a call to NEW with tag field values specified, recycle it by

DISPOSE (*pointer_variable* , *tag1* , *tag2* , ..., *tagN*)

where you have exactly the same number of *tags* as in the call to NEW which allocated the storage, and they have the same values, and moreover those are the tag values that actually occur in the variant record. In summary, always dispose of storage in the same way that you allocated it.

MARK and RELEASE allow bulk recycling of storage, and almost never occur on systems that provide DISPOSE. If you have MARK and RELEASE, storage is allocated sequentially. MARK tells you what the current "high water mark" is, and later you may use RELEASE to recycle all storage allocated since that time.

A call to MARK has the form

MARK (*high_water_mark*)

where *high_water_mark* is some integer variable that you supply. Your program should not modify this variable, and indeed there is little reason ever to use it for anything but a parameter to these routines.

Later, you may reclaim storage by making the call

RELEASE (*high_water_mark*)

where *high_water_mark* is an integer value obtained from some previous call to MARK. The effect is to retain all storage allocated prior to that call to MARK, and to recycle all storage allocated subsequently.

You may, of course, call MARK several times, and keep track of several high-water marks. Generally, however, MARK and RELEASE will be useful only when you want to return to a previous state of the system (say, as part of reinitializing your program to handle a second problem).

Chapter 13

SETS

Sets in mathematics are powerful, flexible, and useful. Pascal has traded most of these virtues for an efficient implementation. The major flaws are

- Many useful sets, such as the set of available characters, often cannot be represented.
- No way is provided to step through all the elements of a set (except in Pascal 8000).
- No input/output of sets is provided, nor is it simple to write your own.
- Use of sets limits program portability, because each implementation permits a different range of elements.

The tragedy is that many programmers may conclude sets have no place in programming, but the true fault lies with the Pascal definition and implementation.

13.1   SET TYPES AND CONSTRUCTORS

A set is defined by

SET OF *base_type*

where the *base_type* may be

- a subrange of the integers;
- a subrange of the characters;
- a user-defined scalar type or subrange thereof, or
- BOOLEAN or a subrange thereof.

The elements of a set must have a numeric representation in the range 0..N, where N is set by the implementation. Typical ranges are

PASLC: 0..71
CDC: 0..58
PASCAL 8000:   0..63
UCSD: 0..511

The numeric representation of an integer is the integer itself. For other types, the numeric representation of their values is given by the ORD of those values.

Set values may be specified by enclosing the elements of the set in square brackets [and] (or their equivalents (. and .) in Pascal 8000). If several consecutive elements are in the set, subrange notation (first..last) may be used. Brackets used in this way are called set constructors.

```
VAR
    PARTS: SET OF 1..20;
    LETTERS: SET OF 'A'..'Z';
    SUBJECTS: SET OF (MATH, HISTORY, ENGLISH, SCIENCE);
BEGIN
    PARTS := [1..5, 7, 15..20, 13, 14];
    LETTERS := ['A'..'M'];
    COURSES := [SCIENCE, MATH];
```

Note that the elements of a set constructor need not appear in any particular order.

The empty set is denoted by [ ]. Use of subrange notation may also result in an empty set, as in [ENGLISH..HISTORY], since the dots behave as an implied FOR loop, with the initial value greater than the final value.

Set constructors may be used for both packed and nonpacked sets. Pascal will figure out from the context which is intended.

If S and T are sets, the following operations are defined.

S + T   Set union: the result is a set containing all the elements that are in S, in T, or in both.

S * T   Set intersection: the result is a set containing those elements that are in both S and T.

S − T   Set difference: the result is a set containing those elements that are in S but not in T.

These operations may be used in conjunction with set constructor notation to add elements to or delete elements from a set, for example,

```
LETTERS := LETTERS + ['Z'];        (* add Z to LETTERS *)
SUBJECTS := SUBJECTS − [MATH];     (* delete MATH from SUBJECTS *)
```

PARTS := PARTS * [1..10];   (* remove parts above 11 *)

Sets may be tested for equality and inclusion with the following relational operators.

S = T   Equality: yields TRUE if S and T are equal, that is, if they have the same elements; else yields FALSE.

S <> T   Inequality: yields TRUE if sets S and T are not equal, FALSE if they are equal.

S <= T   Subset: yields TRUE if every element of S is also a member of T, and FALSE otherwise.

S >= T   Superset: equivalent to T <= S.

The above operations are defined for all sets, so that in theory it is legal to use them even when the sets have different base types, as for example LETTERS + COURSES. Even if your compiler accepts this, the result would be difficult to interpret and to use. Oddly, the operators < and > are not defined on sets.

Finally, Pascal provides the operator IN to test for set membership. If S is a set and X is a value whose type is the same as the base type of the set, then X IN S returns TRUE if X is an element of S, FALSE if it is not. X IN S is equivalent to [X] <= S.

An easy slip to make is to write X NOT IN S as the negation of X IN S. This is illegal, because NOT and IN are operators (although they are written as words), and you cannot juxtapose operators. The correct form is NOT (X IN S), and it must be written with parentheses.

13.2 USING SETS

Pascal sets are useful when you wish to attach a binary (yes/no) attribute to a small, known set of objects or values. For example, you might keep a schedule of busy evenings as follows.

```
TYPE
      DAYS = (SUN, MON, TUE, WED, THU, FRI, SAT);
VAR
      EVENING: DAYS;
      BOOKED: SET OF DAYS;
. . .
IF EVENING IN BOOKED THEN WRITE(' SORRY.')
ELSE BOOKED:=BOOKED+[EVENING];
```

Pascal sets are also useful for classifying characters (and sometimes other data types) into groups.

CH IN ['0'..'9']	tests if CH is a digit,
CH IN ['[', ']']	tests if CH is a bracket,
EVENING IN [FRI, SAT]	tests if the next day is a work day.

Before you write programs which use this feature to classify characters, however, you should make sure that the characters you are interested in can legally occur in sets, that is, their code in the collating sequence is sufficiently low.

It is possible to sequence through all the elements of a set. We first give the Pascal 8000 construct for doing this, then show how that construct can be kludged in other Pascals. The syntax is

FORALL *variable* IN *set_expression* DO *statement*

where

set_expression is any expression resulting in a set,

variable is a simple identifier whose type is the same as the base type of the *set_expression*, and

statement is any single statement.

Upon completion of the loop, the *variable* becomes undefined.

Examples:

```
FORALL EVENING IN BOOKED DO
    ENJOY(EVENING);

PRIMESUM: = 0;
FORALL N IN PRIMES DO
    BEGIN
    WRITELN(N, ' IS A PRIME.');
    PRIMESUM: = PRIMESUM + N
    END;
```

The FORALL loop can be simulated in other Pascals by looping through all possible values of the base set and, for each such value, testing whether it actually occurs in the set.

```
FOR EVENING: = SUN TO SAT DO
    IF EVENING IN BOOKED THEN ENJOY(EVENING);

PRIMESUM: = 0;
FOR N: = 0 TO 50 DO
    IF N IN PRIMES THEN
        BEGIN
        WRITELN(N, ' IS A PRIME.');
```

```
PRIMESUM: = PRIMESUM + N
END;
```

A set may not be read from or written to a textfile, because Pascal does not know how you want a set represented as a string of characters. However, it is relatively easy to write your own input/output routines for sets, especially if the base type of the set (the type of elements in it) can easily be input and output. A set of user-defined scalars is more difficult to input and output simply because user-defined scalars are themselves difficult to input and output.

In the following code, we assume that sets are represented externally by a simple list of their values, enclosed in brackets and separated by commas. To input a set of integers,

```
REPEAT READ(CH) UNTIL CH = '[';
REPEAT
      READ(N):
      INTSET: = INTSET + [N];
      REPEAT READ(CH) UNTIL (CH = ',') OR (CH = ']')
UNTIL CH = ']';
```

This code unfortunately fails for the empty set, [ ]. Pascal always has to know the type of the thing it is about to read, so we can do this by alternating characters (',' or ']') with integers; in fact, this is why we decided to use commas between elements. The problem is not an easy one to solve; see Section 12.5 for some hints on reading arbitrary input.

It is always a good idea to make input and output formats compatible, so that something written out by a program may later be read in by some program. With this in mind, our output routine uses brackets and commas— but the code is a bit tricky.

```
FIRST: = TRUE;
WRITE(' [');
FORALL N IN INTSET DO
      BEGIN
      IF FIRST THEN FIRST: = FALSE ELSE WRITE(',');
      WRITE(N);
      END;
WRITELN(']');
```

This code uses the FORALL construct, which can easily be replaced as described above. It will print out the empty set correctly, as [ ].

Appendix A

SUMMARY OF DECLARATION SECTIONS AND STATEMENT TYPES

Comments give relevant section numbers in the text.

PROGRAM *program_name* (*list_of_files*);   (* 8.1, 8.2 *)

LABEL
    list_of_labels;   (* 3.1 *)

CONST
    identifier = *value*;   (* 3.2 *)

TYPE
    type_name = *type*;   (* 3.3 *)

VAR
    list_of_names: *type*;   (* 3.4 *)

VALUE
    variable := *constant*;   (* Pascal 8000 only—3.5 *)

```
PROCEDURE procedure_name (VAR list_of_formal_parameters: type_name;
                              list_of_formal_parameters:  type_name);
        declarations;                                       (* 7.1–7.7 *)
        BEGIN
            sequence_of_statements
        END;

PROCEDURE procedure_name_2 (parameters); FORWARD;           (* 7.5 *)

FUNCTION function_name (parameters): result_type;           (* 7.1 *)
        declarations;
        BEGIN
            sequence_of_statements;
                function_name := value                      (* 7.4 *)
        END;

PROCEDURE procedure_name_2;               (* parameters not repeated *)
        declarations;
        BEGIN
            sequence_of_statements
        END;



BEGIN   (* -------- Main program -------- *)
        variable := expression;                             (* 4.5 *)

        BEGIN (* Compound statement *)                      (* 1.3 *)
            sequence_of_statements
        END;

        CASE expression OF                                  (* 5.2 *)
            list_of_constants: statement;
            list_of_constants: statement
        END;

        FOR variable := initial_value TO final_value DO     (* 6.4 *)
            statement;

        FOR variable := initial_value DOWNTO final_value DO (* 6.4 *)
            statement;

        FORALL variable IN set_expression DO   (* Pascal 8000 only—13.2 *)
            statement;

        label: GOTO label;                                  (* 3.1 *)

        IF condition THEN                                   (* 5.1 *)
            statement;
```

IF *condition* THEN   (* 5.1 *)
    statement
ELSE
    statement;

LOOP   (* Pascal 8000 only—6.5 *)
    sequence_of_statements   (* may contain EXIT *)
END;

LOOP UNTIL *list_of_events*:   (* Pascal 8000 only—6.5 *)
    sequence_of_statements   (* each event is a statement *)
POSTLUDE
    event: *statement*;
    event: *statement*
END;

LOOP   (* PASLC only—6.6 *)
    sequence_of_statements
EXIT IF *condition*;
    sequence_of_statements
END;

procedure_name (*list_of_actual_parameters*);   (* 7.2 *)

REPEAT   (* 6.3 *)
    sequence_of_statements
UNTIL *condition*;

WHILE *condition* DO   (* 6.2 *)
    statement;

WITH *list_of_records* DO *statement*   (* 12.6 *)
END.   (* 1.1 *)

Appendix B

BUILT-IN FUNCTIONS AND PROCEDURES

The following is an alphabetical list of built-in functions and procedures supplied by Pascal, along with a reference to the proper section in which to look for further information. Not all of these functions and procedures will be present in any given implementation. Those which are part of Standard Pascal, and therefore ought to be present in any given implementation, are marked with a star (*). Parameters which may be changed by the call are marked with the keyword VAR.

* FUNCTION	ABS(*integer*): *integer*	(* 4.1 *)
	ABS(*real*): *real*	(* 4.1 *)
* FUNCTION	ARCTAN(*real*): *real*	(* 4.1 *)
FUNCTION	ATAN(*real*): *real*	(* 4.1 *)
PROCEDURE	BREAK	(* 8.7 *)
* FUNCTION	CHR(*integer*): *char*	(* 11.1 *)
PROCEDURE	CLOSE(*file*)	(* 8.2 *)
	CLOSE(*file*, CRUNCH)	(* 8.2 *)
	CLOSE(*file*, LOCK)	(* 8.2 *)
	CLOSE(*file*, NORMAL)	(* 8.2 *)
	CLOSE(*file*, PURGE)	(* 8.2 *)
FUNCTION	CONCAT(*string*, ..., *string*): *string*	(* 11.3 *)
FUNCTION	COPY(*string, integer, integer*): *string*	(* 11.3 *)

* FUNCTION	COS(*real*): *real*	(* 4.1 *)
PROCEDURE	DELETE(VAR *string, count, count*)	(* 11.3 *)
* PROCEDURE	DISPOSE(*pointer*)	(* 12.7 *)
	DISPOSE(*pointer, tag, ..., tag*)	(* 12.7 *)
* FUNCTION	EOF: *boolean*	(* 8.5 *)
	EOF(*file*): *boolean*	(* 8.5 *)
* FUNCTION	EOLN: *boolean*	(* 8.5 *)
	EOLN(*textfile*): *boolean*	(* 8.5 *)
FUNCTION	EOS(*file*): *boolean*	(* 8.8 *)
PROCEDURE	EXIT(PROGRAM)	(* 7.1 *)
	EXIT(*routine_name*)	(* 7.1 *)
FUNCTION	EXP(*real*): *real*	(* 4.1 *)
* PROCEDURE	GET	(* 8.6 *)
	GET(*file*)	(* 8.6 *)
PROCEDURE	GETSEG(*file*)	(* 8.8 *)
	GETSEG(*file, number_of_segments*)	(* 8.8 *)
PROCEDURE	INSERT(*string*, VAR *string, index*)	(* 11.3 *)
FUNCTION	LENGTH(*string*): *integer*	(* 11.3 *)
* FUNCTION	LN(*real*): *real*	(* 4.1 *)
PROCEDURE	MARK(VAR *integer*)	(* 12.7 *)
* PROCEDURE	NEW(VAR *pointer*)	(* 12.7 *)
	NEW(VAR *pointer, tag, ..., tag*)	(* 12.7 *)
* FUNCTION	ODD(*integer*): *boolean*	(* 4.2 *)
* FUNCTION	ORD(*boolean*): *integer*	(* 4.2 *)
	ORD(*char*): *integer*	(* 11.1 *)
	ORD(*integer*): *integer*	(* 6.4 *)
	ORD(*enumeration*): *integer*	(* 9.1 *)
* PROCEDURE	PACK(*array, integer*, VAR *packed_array*)	(* 11.2 *)
* PROCEDURE	PAGE	(* 8.3 *)
	PAGE(*textfile*)	(* 8.3 *)
FUNCTION	POS(*string, string*): *integer*	(* 11.3 *)
* FUNCTION	PRED(*char*): *char*	(* 11.1 *)
	PRED(*enumeration*): *enumeration*	(* 9.1 *)
* PROCEDURE	PUT	(* 8.6 *)
	PUT(*file*)	(* 8.6 *)
PROCEDURE	PUTSEG(*file*)	(* 8.8 *)
* PROCEDURE	READ	(* 8.3 *)
	READ(*file*)	(* 8.3 *)
	READ(*file*, VAR *list_of_variables*)	(* 8.3 *)
	READ(VAR *list_of_variables*)	(* 8.3 *)

* PROCEDURE	READLN	(* 8.3 *)
	READLN(*file*)	(* 8.3 *)
	READLN(*file*, VAR *list_of_variables*)	(* 8.3 *)
	READLN(VAR *list_of_variables*)	(* 8.3 *)
PROCEDURE	RELEASE(*integer*)	(* 12.7 *)
* PROCEDURE	RESET(*file*)	(* 8.2, 8.6 *)
	RESET(*file*, *string*)	(* 8.2 *)
* PROCEDURE	REWRITE(*file*)	(* 8.2, 8.6 *)
	REWRITE(*file*, *integer*)	(* 8.8 *)
	REWRITE(*file*, *string*)	(* 8.2 *)
* FUNCTION	ROUND(*real*): *integer*	(* 4.5 *)
* FUNCTION	SIN(*real*): *real*	(* 4.1 *)
* FUNCTION	SQR(*integer*): *integer*	(* 4.1 *)
	SQR(*real*): *real*	(* 4.1 *)
* FUNCTION	SQRT(*real*): *real*	(* 4.1 *)
PROCEDURE	STR(*integer*, VAR *string*)	(* 11.3 *)
	STR(*long integer*, VAR *string*)	(* 11.3 *)
* FUNCTION	SUCC(*char*): *char*	(* 11.1 *)
	SUCC(*enumeration*): *enumeration*	(* 9.1 *)
* FUNCTION	TRUNC(*real*): *integer*	(* 4.5 *)
* PROCEDURE	UNPACK(*packed_array*, *integer*, VAR *array*)	(* 11.2 *)
* PROCEDURE	WRITE	(* 8.3 *)
	WRITE(*list*)	(* 8.3 *)
	WRITE(*list_of_expressions*)	(* 8.3 *)
	WRITE(*file*, *list_of_expressions*)	(* 8.3 *)
* PROCEDURE	WRITELN	(* 8.3 *)
	WRITELN(*file*)	(* 8.3 *)
	WRITELN(*list_of_expressions*)	(* 8.3 *)
	WRITELN(*file*, *list_of_expressions*)	(* 8.3 *)

Appendix C

COLLATING SEQUENCES

DISPLAY CODE (FOR CDC 6000-3.4 PASCAL)

0 *eoln*	16 P	32 5	48 $\equiv$
1 A	17 Q	33 6	49 [
2 B	18 R	34 7	50]
3 C	19 S	35 8	51 :
4 D	20 T	36 9	52 $=$
5 E	21 U	37 +	53 $\rightarrow$
6 F	22 V	38 -	54 $\vee$
7 G	23 W	39 $*$	55 $\wedge$
8 H	24 X	40 /	56 $\uparrow$
9 I	25 Y	41 (	57 $\downarrow$
10 J	26 Z	42)	58 $<$
11 K	27 0	43 $	59 $>$
12 L	28 1	44 $=$	60 $\leq$
13 M	29 2	45 *blank*	61 $\geq$
14 N	30 3	46 ,	62 $\neg$
15 O	31 4	47 .	63 ;

STANDARD EBCDIC (FOR PASCAL 8000)

0	NUL	44		88		132	d
1	SOH	45	ENQ	89		133	e
2	STX	46	ACK	90	!	134	f
3	ETX	47	BEL	91	$	135	g
4	PF	48		92	*	136	h
5	HT	49		93	)	137	i
6	LC	50	SYN	94	;	138	
7	DEL	51		95	⌐	139	
8		52	PN	96	-	140	
9		53	RS	97	/	141	
10	SMM	54	UC	98		142	
11	VT	55	EOT	99		143	
12	FF	56		100		144	
13	CR	57		101		145	j
14	SO	58		102		146	k
15	SI	59	CU3	103		147	l
16	DLE	60	DC4	104		148	m
17	DC1	61	NAK	105		149	n
18	DC2	62		106			150	r
19	TM	63	SUB	107	,	151	
20	RES	64	blank	108	%	152	
21	NL	65		109	—	153	
22	BS	66		110	>	154	
23	IL	67		111	?	155	
24	CAN	68		112		156	
25	EM	69		113		157	
26	CC	70		114		158	
27	CU1	71		115		159	
28	IFS	72		116		160	
29	IGS	73		117		161	~
30	IRS	74	¢	118		162	s
31	IUS	75	.	119		163	t
32	DS	76	<	120		164	u
33	SOS	77	(	121	`	165	v
34	FS	78	+	122	:	166	w
35		79			123	#	167	x
36	BYP	80	&	124	@	168	y
37	LF	81		125	'	169	z
38	ETB	82		126	=	170	
39	ESC	83		127	"	171	
40		84		128		172	
41		85		129	a	173	
42	SM	86		130	b	174	
43	CU2	87		131	c	175	

176		196	D	216	Q	237	
177		197	E	217	R	238	
178		198	F	219		239	
179		199	G	220		240	0
180		200	H	221		241	1
181		201	I	222		242	2
182		202		223		243	3
183		203		224	\	244	4
184		204		225		245	5
185		205		226	S	246	6
186		206		227	T	247	7
187		207		228	U	248	8
188		208		229	V	249	9
189		209	J	230	W	250	|
190		210	K	231	X	251	
191		211	L	232	Y	252	
192	{	212	M	233	Z	253	
193	A	213	N	234		254	
194	B	214	O	235		255	
195	C	215	P	236			

ASCII (FOR UCSD PASCAL AND PASLC)

0 NUL	32 blank	64 @	96
1 SOH	33 !	65 A	97 a
2 STX	34 "	66 B	98 b
3 ETX	35 #	67 C	99 c
4 EOT	36 $	68 D	100 d
5 ENQ	37 %	69 E	101 e
6 ACK	38 &	70 F	102 f
7 BEL	39 ´	71 G	103 g
8 BS	40 (	72 H	104 h
9 HT	41)	73 I	105 i
10 LF	42 *	74 J	106 j
11 VT	43 +	75 K	107 k
12 FF	44 ,	76 L	108 l
13 CR	45 -	77 M	109 m
14 SO	46 .	78 N	110 n
15 SI	47 /	79 O	111 o
16 DLE	48 0	80 P	112 p
17 DC1	49 1	81 Q	113 q
18 DC2	50 2	82 R	114 r
19 DC3	51 3	83 S	115 s
20 DC4	52 4	84 T	116 t
21 NAK	53 5	85 U	117 u
22 SYN	54 6	86 V	118 v
23 ETB	55 7	87 W	119 w
24 CAN	56 8	88 X	120 x
25 EM	57 9	89 Y	121 y
26 SUB	58 :	90 Z	122 z
27 ESC	59 ;	91 [	123 {
28 FS	60 <	92 \	124 |
29 GS	61 =	93]	125 }
30 RS	62 >	94 ^	126 ~
31 US	63 ?	95 —	127 DEL

Appendix D

COMPILER OPTIONS

UCSD PASCAL

Syntax: (*$*option*,...,*option**)

Options available.

(*$C *text**)	Insert *text* into codefile (intended for copyright notices.)
(*$G + *)	Allow GOTO statements.
(*$G − *)	Disallow GOTO statements (default).
(*$I + *)	Insert error checks after I/O (default).
(*$I − *)	Do not check if I/O was successful.
(*$I *file**)	Copy (include) the name *file* into the program at this point.
(*$L + *)	Save listing as SYSTEM.LST.TEXT.
(*$L − *)	Do not list program (default).
(*$L *file**)	Save listing as the specified *file*.
(*$N + *)	Load UNIT only when active.
(*$N − *)	Load UNIT when program begins (default).
(*$P*)	Insert form feed into listing at this point.
(*$Q + *)	Compile quietly (without messages).
(*$Q − *)	Show progress of compilation (default).
(*$R + *)	Check array and string subscripts, and assignments to subrange types (default).

(*$R − *)   Do not check ranges and subscripts.

(*$R *name**)   Keep the *named* UNIT or SEGMENT resident in memory (do not swap).

(*$S + *)   Swap portions of compiler in and out as needed. Increases space, slows compiler.

(*$S − *)   Do no swapping with compiler (default).

(*$S + + *)   Do lots of swapping.

(*$U + *)   Compile as user program (default).

(*$U − *)   Compile as systems program. Sets G +, I −, R −.

(*$U *file**)   Use the named *file* as the library.

PASCAL 8000

Syntax: (*$*option*,...,*option comment**)

Options available.

(*$C + *)   List object code.

(*$C − *)   Do not list object code (default).

(*$L + *)   List program (default).

(*$L − *)   Do not list program.

(*$N + *)   Produce traceback on error.

(*$N − *)   Do not produce traceback on error (default).

(*$P + *)   Produce postmortem dump on error (default).

(*$P − *)   Do not produce dump on error.

(*$T + *)   Do runtime error checking (default).

(*$T − *)   Do not generate runtime error checks.

(*$S + *)   Flag all constructs not in Standard Pascal.

(*$S − *)   Do not flag nonstandard constructs (default).

(*$U + *)   Compile only first 72 characters of each line.

(*$U − *)   Compile up to 120 chars/line (default).

PASLC AND RELATED DEC-10 COMPILERS

Syntax: (*$*option*,...,*option**)

Options available.

(*$C + *)   Do runtime error checking (default).

(*$C − *)   Do not generate error-checking code.

(∗$L + ∗)   List the object code.
(∗$L − ∗)   Do not list the object code (default).

(∗$T + ∗)   Open TTY when program begins (default).
(∗$T − ∗)   Do not automatically open TTY.

CDC PASCAL 6000-3.4

Syntax: (∗$*option*,...,*option comment*∗)

Options available.

(∗$B*digit*∗)   Make file buffers at least 128∗*digit* words long (default = B1).

(∗$E + ∗)   Use first 7 characters of each external name.
(∗$E − ∗)   Generate internal names for modules (default).

(∗$L + ∗)   List the program (default).
(∗$L − ∗)   Do not list the program.

(∗$P + ∗)   Provide postmortem dump on error (default).
(∗$P − ∗)   Do not provide postmortem dump.

(∗$T + ∗)   Include runtime error tests (default).
(∗$T − ∗)   Do not include runtime error tests.

(∗$U + ∗)   Compile only first 72 columns.
(∗$U − ∗)   Compile up to 120 columns (default).

(∗$X*digit*∗)   Pass parameters in registers X0 to X*digit* (default = X4).

INDEX

173